HOW TO LET IT GO

HOW TO LET IT GO

An Inspiational Journey to Eliminate
Negative Emotions and Limiting Beliefs

~

Creating Awareness of M.E.R.®
(Mental Emotional Release) -

Your Road to Self-Empowerment,
True Happiness and Living a Life Filled with Passion & Purpose

LIANA GOFFMAN

A GIFT FOR YOU

A Complimentary Audio Addition is available with the purchase or download of a print or e-book.

Go to:

www.LetitGo-MER.com/Audiobook_FDL

In an effort to support our local communities and raise awareness of MER°, Liana donates a percentage of all book sales to various charities affiliated with trauma victims, veterans with PTSD, along with raped, battered, and trafficked women.

All stories in this book are based on real people, however, names and situations may have been changed to protect their identity.

Disclaimer

Because of the technological nature of the Internet, any web addresses or links contained in this book may have changed

What you get by achieving your goals is
not as important as what you become by
achieving your goals."

~ Henry David Thoreau

Dedication:

This book is dedicated to all my friends and family who have helped and supported me throughout my journey towards self empowerment. I understand and accept that I may not have been the best or easiest person to be around during the dark times in my life and I may have unknowingly hurt or disappointed you in my efforts to pick myself up or even get through the day. I feel truly blessed and fortunate that I have been given the opportunity to request forgiveness and make it up to each and every one of you. I give credit to the Empowerment Partnership, their educational programs, assistants, and guidance in their pursuit to help me turn my life around. I thank my editors, designers, promoters, FB friends and mastermind group members in helping me produce and create a quality product. An extra special and personal thank you goes out to my mom, who after 50 years has finally become my best friend and my rock. Without her physical, financial, mental, emotional, and spiritual support, patience, and love, the publication of this book would never be possible. This book will allow me to spread awareness of the amazingly successful NLP tools of MER® which will be utilized in my newfound passion of helping others break out of being stuck from their own past traumas and negative experiences. My goal is to give others the ability to finally take their first step into the light of passion and positivity. I love you all!

2. If you don't ask, the answer will always be no.

Human nature is averse to pain and discomfort.
We want everything to be smooth But we don't grow
from staying still.
We don't bring our dreams alive by playing it safe.
We don't get what we want by waiting for God to
deliver it to your doorstep.
We must embrace difficulty and change if we are to
create a fulfilling life for ourselves.

If the boat is not rocking, it's not going anywhere.

Kaballah - Karen Berg

Index

You are not what others think you are. You are what God knows you are. ~ Shannon L. Alder

The size of greatness inside of you is measured
by the challenges you overcome.

Yehuda Berg

Intro

~Letter to my Readers~

Dear Reader-

I'm writing this book to let you know that there is someone out here who understands the frustration, apathy, anger, sadness, fear, hurt or guilt that you are feeling. Over many years, I have felt and became overwhelmed by all of these negative feelings. In just a few short months (three to be exact) my life became so overwhelming, I was diagnosed with PTSD[1] - Post Traumatic Stress Disorder from more than five different traumatic events that occurred in my past. I went to a dark place with such apathy that I felt if I didn't take immediate action, my now happy and amazing life, could have become a downward spiral leading to my possible death. I thank Dr. Matt and the Empowerment Partnership for helping me out of this dark place.

For some of you, there may be an ounce of purpose... you may have children that rely on you, a husband or wife who loves you, an elderly or ageing parent that needs your help... for now, that may be your only "why" for existing. But, what happens if you are all alone? No wife or husband, no kids, your parents are either distant, or content without your involvement, busy with their own lives, or have already passed. That was me...

Before I was officially diagnosed with these five traumatic PTSD events, I didn't know where to turn, or who to turn to. I was stuck. If you have somehow reached that place of "why" and you are searching for your path, trying to regain some type of purpose for your existence or lost your passion along the way... then this book is for you!

Deep in the depths of your soul, there is a reason for living. The conscious mind may not know what it is, but, if you think back to when you were a kid without conscious limits, anything was possible. Most likely a teacher, relative, or parent once said, "You can be whatever you want to be, when you grow up," and then asked, "What do YOU want to do or be when YOU grow up?" Maybe you paused, thought for a moment, and then blurted out something that filled your heart with joy and excitement. You may or may not consciously remember that exact moment when it happened, but think about a small child that you know who dresses up as a fireman, or who won't take off that princess dress or superhero cape. They truly believe they ARE that princess or superhero!

Along the road of life with all its different paths, roads, hills, valleys and turns, a lot of us got off track or "got

I am encouraged by the positive change I can make in my life, regardless of how small or insignificant it may seem at the moment.

stuck". This was mostly by no fault of our own, but due to accidents, sickness, family, environment, finances, friends, and at the moment a specific choice. Things happened. Things came up. Either something or someone got in the way. Perhaps they presented you with a different or what seemed like a better option, and we based our decision on how to proceed by what felt good at the time. We did not think or know if it was potentially the wrong or right path, a longer or shorter route... and along the way, something happened... an unexpected experience, an unexpected trauma, an undesirable situation. This affected the central nervous system and caused a negative emotion.

How did you respond? Did you respond, or did you react? Did you ignore it, as if it didn't occur? Did you do something to try and get past it? What happened when that block in the road became so big that when you tried and tried you couldn't get around it, over it, under it or even get through it?

Now, think back into your life. Is there anything from your past that you still can't shake off or just let go of? Something that triggers unwarranted outbursts of anger or tears? What is that particular negative emotion that YOU are still holding onto? Is there more than one?

Have you ever just decided that reaching a particular goal or perhaps the end result of that particular goal wasn't really worth the effort anymore? You went

The older you get, the more you realize that it isn't about the material things, or pride or ego. It's about our hearts and who they beat for.

through all the motions, and in your mind, you thought that you tried and tried but you still didn't seem to be moving forward? Or, you waited for that block to go away and then forgot where you were originally headed towards in the first place? These roadblocks can either put you on the wrong track, the long track, or just take you off the track completely. So, no matter where you are right now, if you don't know, or can't remember your "WHY", your "PURPOSE", your "PASSION"... If you have lost that little voice inside of your head saying, "You can do whatever you want, and you can be whoever you want to be," then, this book is for you!

If you're feeling even a little stuck, or you feel that something or someone has done something "TO YOU" that you feel has "hurt you" or limited your ability to move on, or you have decided to put up a block, then, this book is for you.

Now if you've read several "self-help" books, you've posted affirmations on the bathroom mirror, and you've given up on traditional therapy or counselors who just keep asking you to talk about YOUR Story... If you are lost in your own head, holding onto a limited belief, you cannot imagine your life getting infinitely better, and you don't know where to go or who to turn to... then this book is for you!

In this book, I reveal the number one (1) missing link from "The Secret", and what the "Self-help" speakers and

An arrow can only be shot by pulling it backward. When life is dragging you back, just imagine that it's going to launch you into something great!

gurus have left out.

Have you repeatedly told Traditional Psychiatrists and Therapists your story, only to leave their offices feeling worse than when you walked in? Have they promised that the law of attraction, positive thinking and posting affirmations will help you to reach your goals? Have you become frustrated? Why has nothing you've tried in the past worked for YOU? Why does it seem to work for everyone else? Have you ever asked yourself, "WHY NOT ME?"

Are you ready for the answer?

Now, all these tools really can work for everyone BUT, if your unconscious mind is doing its job, trying to protect you, then unconsciously it will continue to bring up what your conscious mind has learned from your past.

Throughout your life you have come to believe your truths based on experiences. You remember experiences based on the emotions that experience had provoked. Once you have experienced a negative emotion causing event, your mind will bring up those negative thoughts in its attempt to remind and protect you. This limited perception sometimes causes an overwhelming reaction of negative thoughts, regrets, or feelings from these previous paths you have chosen.

So, how do you expect to stay positive when those old negative beliefs and feelings keep getting in the way?

If you want to change the world, go home and love your family. ~ Mother Teresa

The KEY is to First, remove and disassociate any and all of your negative emotions such as anger, sadness, fear, hurt, guilt at the root cause. And Second, remove all of your limiting beliefs and decisions that you have made in your past.

Let me say that again... **It is the absolute most important lesson in this book and your first introduction to MER®2.**

> **The KEY is to First, remove and disassociate any and all of your negative emotions such as anger, sadness, fear, hurt, guilt at the root cause. And Second, remove all of your limiting beliefs and decisions that you have made in your past.**

We call this MER® (Mental and Emotional Release). Once you learn the lesson, disassociate from the event, eliminate the negative triggers, you can then better identify your personal values, prioritize them, and then create several sets of S.M.A.R.T[3].   Goals that will help put you back on track to navigate you towards the life you have always wanted and the goals that are in place.

Think of a time when you got in a fight with a friend, parent, sibling or child... Go in your mind's eye to a specific time. Now, try to remember the feeling of emotional anger you had? In your imagination, try to relive that moment as if it was right now. See what you saw, hear what you heard, feel what you felt. Remember being there in that moment... what were you feeling?

Did that feeling go on for a long time?

Now think about when you decided to forgive them... At the actual moment when you decided to forgive them. Can you remember how long were you still angry or upset?

Think about it... Once you made the decision to not be angry, how long did that take to feel better? It was instantaneous! Wasn't it? Wow!

We really do have this amazing ability to remove the residual negative feelings (like anger) instantaneously. Now you just need to be properly guided through the process of MER® to eliminate all those additional pent up and stuck negative emotions and limiting beliefs that you have been carrying around with you for so long... Most likely since childhood.

Of course, it is a little more complicated than this, but I'm giving you a quick preview as to how quickly you can start your new life and take the necessary steps to begin feeling unstuck immediately.

The process of MER® is a way to disassociate yourself from a particular event that triggered a specific emotion. Once disassociated from that event and the emotional response it caused, all the following or future unwarranted emotions (heightened emotional outbursts that are out of proportion with the current situation) can be cleared to no longer create that

life is too short to spend time with people who suck the happiness out of you.

emotional charge or those negative feelings. Once you can look back at an event as if you were watching it on TV or in an old movie, you unconsciously stop feeling the need to continually carry that negative emotion or limiting belief around with you. You no longer need that protection from experiencing that emotion. You have learned the lesson and now, as an adult, have a much better understanding of how to deal with those types of particular events. That is why a lot of people use the term "baggage". For example, if deep down you believe that "money is the root of all evil," and wealthy people are evil, then no matter how many times you say to yourself, "money flows easily and effortlessly into my life," you may never truly believe it or be able to attract it. First you must eliminate that negative and limiting belief surrounding money and wealthy people.

Once you allow your unconscious mind to "let go" of all the limiting beliefs, then, and only then, can you start deeply believing in everything those positive affirmations have been telling you. What you just read, IS the missing link.

After my own personal breakthrough, I had assisted in some trainings. These were the same trainings that I sat in while trying to get myself unstuck. I told some of the participants my story of going from rock bottom to living a fulfilling life in the place of my dreams. I went from feeling total despair and misery, to living a passionate and purposeful life. I went from not wanting

Lord grant me the serenity to accept stupid people the way they are, courage to maintain my self control and the wisdom to know that if I act on it, I will go to jail.

to get out of bed, to becoming an advocate for others trying to overcome their own personal challenges. I was told time and time again how inspirational and motivational my story was to them and how I impacted their decisions to move forward.

As a result, this encouragement from so many to tell my story inspired me to write this book, share my journey, inspire others, and share the many lessons I have learned. Until now, not very many people know or share the missing link to success, and those who do know it, use it daily. My teacher says that we are all like onions, we need to peel off the daily crap that goes on in our heads, forgive those around us for not knowing any better, become "at cause" for our actions, thoughts, decisions, and feelings, learn our lessons, and once we have accomplished all that, we are then able to feel complete, with a sense of positive self awareness and wellbeing. Then, and only then, can we live the passionate and purposeful life we were all meant to live.

We call this EMPOWERMENT.

The life you have always dreamt about and deeply desire is waiting for you.

So, let's start you on your journey to empowerment today!

Today, resist judgment, let go of your pride and entitlement, and make room for the Creator to work miracles on your behalf.

Let me too you something you already know.
The world ain't all sunshine and rainbows. I
t's a very mean and nasty place and I don't care how
tough you are it will beat you to your knees and keep
you there permanently if you let it.
You, me, or nobody is gonna hit as hard as life.
Bit it ain't about how hard ya hit. It's about how hard
you can get hit and keep moving forward.
How much you an take and keep moving forward.
That's how winning is done!

~ Sylvester Stallone, Rocky Balboa

Gratitude unlocks the fullness of life. It turns what we have into enough, and more. Gratitude makes sense of our past, brings peace for today, and creates a vision for tomorrow. - Melody Beattie

How to Let it Go!

10

Prologue

~Who am I?~

I, Liana Goffman, Author, Real Estate Broker, Master Negotiation Expert, Master Practitioner in NLP[4], MER®, and Hypnosis, hold several designations and I am continually educating myself to pursue more knowledge of the world around me. I've never quite felt like an expert at anything, even with multiple designations and certificates, I continued to struggle for many years until one day... several years after my father passed, I lay in bed and felt the cool breeze of the ceiling fan wisp across my stubbly unshaven legs. I stared up at the spinning blades of the ceiling fan, feeling the back of my head rest against the soft pillow and started my evening meditation.

I paused, took in a deep breath and closed my eyes, looking at the light within my mind... you know those colorful moving shapes and squiggles on the inside of your eyelids.

Try it. Close your eyes (while you are in the dark) look up between your eyes toward the middle of your forehead (you may feel your eyelids flutter a bit) and then relax... focus on the movement of the changing shapes and colors that are deep within. Try not to let your mind wander, just focus on the light and on your breath. This is how I connect to my higher self. I believe that the light inside our body is our connection to God, to our soul and to our higher self. It's almost like when you close your eyes and face directly into the sun, all those little bright speckles that shine inside your eyelids. I try to imagine that is when nature is healing me cell by cell.

This one particular evening, I went to my place of relaxation and in a calm, unknowing, curious and almost desperate cry for help, I wondered...

Why? Why am I here? For what purpose? God, what do you want me to do in this lifetime?

I had finally asked the question and now there was no turning back.

Why is there no road map, why am I so unhappy, what do I need to do to get out of this slump? What do I really care about?

I paused again, took in another deep breath... and couldn't answer my own questions. It was at that very moment, I decided I would have to search for the answers.

I turned over, pulled the covers up over my head, and quickly fell asleep... off into dreamland, probably my favorite place to be. The ONLY place I thought that I could have EVERYTHING I had always wanted, go everyplace my heart could imagine and fulfill my every desire. I could taste all the amazing flavors of different foods and drinks, experience the feelings of being adored by handsome men, and I always looked like a perfect model... just like those glamorous women in the high fashion clothing magazines. My internal dream's vision was incredible and always positive. I was able to feel free, do and accomplish everything successfully, go anywhere, attract anyone, and look amazing in any outfit, even in a tiny sexy bikini.

Every night I went on some new and different adventure, sometimes visiting similar places with familiar people, and sometimes in a totally different imaginary wonderful world. Places that were almost recognizable as if I had maybe seen them before in a movie, a photo, possibly in a past life, or lost someplace in my unconscious mind from something I saw in childhood.

While you sit or lay there reading this book, feeling your back against the chair, sofa, or bed, I want you to think back. Try and remember one or more of your special "KODAK" moments. Visualize an amazingly vivid or wacky TV ad, the illustrations in those cute Dr. Seuss books, or how your mind envisioned a poem or greeting card when you read it for the first time.

You don't always need a plan. Sometimes you just need to breathe, trust, let go, and see what happens.

~ Mandy Hale

I loved my dreams. I looked forward to going to sleep every night and anticipated the feelings and sounds of what could happen to me next. This evening, I was experiencing tasting delicious foods, a fresh, crispy shelled, shrimp tostada with a squeeze of lime and a touch of avocado. All while visiting one of my favorite pool bars, at our family vacation spot in Cabo... I traveled all over... and joining me were my personal entourage of best friends, and adoring men. Tonight, I ended up walking arm in arm with my soul mate, toes touching the sand, smelling the salt air and listening to the pounding waves crash and roll upon the shore. I felt loved and adored as I stretched up on my tippy toes for a passionate kiss in the mist of a splash that tickled my cheek.

I just continued to lay there in my bed and take it all in. I enjoyed seeing the sites, smelling the smells, and tasting the fabulous flavors. What a way to enjoy life... never wanting to wake up!

"BEEP, BEEP, BEEP!"... the alarm going off would pull me out of my steamy, hot summer day fantasies or evening, lazy river relaxing escapades...

I would slowly wipe off the sparkling from the sun, sexy, beads of sweat, and set down my deliciously decorated with fruit and a fancy umbrella cocktail. The handsome men would wave their goodbyes, I would reach up, take a deep breath, yawn and stretch... thinking to myself, "I cannot wait until tonight... or the next time I will be able to crawl back into bed and return to paradise."

"BEEP, BEEP, BEEP!" I then opened my eyes, reached over, and turned off the alarm.

This morning was different, the apathy was almost paralyzing. All I wanted to do was turn over and return to my own little world of paradise where everything was good and I was happy. I thought, how can my dream life be SO much better than my reality?

What can I do to change my reality?

I didn't even have the energy to get up and interact with friends, colleagues, or family throughout the day. I knew, as it has always been the same, the common response from friends or family was, "this is it," enjoy and appreciate what you have, it could be worse!

Yes, I knew it could be worse... and deep down I also knew it could be better. Where was my passion? Where was my drive? How and when did all my goals and aspirations get squashed...?

As a kid, not only was anything and everything possible, my desires were pure, my energy was strong, my intentions were caring and positive, I thought like all kids, that I was invincible and there was no way anything could stop me from achieving my dreams. I could be a princess, a president, anything I thought sounded fun or interesting.

Make your life a masterpiece; imagine no limitations on what you can be, have or do. ~ Brian Tracy

"God," I thought and asked aloud, "what is my purpose, am I here for a reason?" I paused, remembering a past conversation I had with an old friend... If the goal is to go to heaven, I felt ready! Take me...

It wasn't as though at that moment I was suicidal or anything, I just thought that if I could go to sleep and never wake up, I would be content to stay in this perfect, imaginary, dream heaven for eternity. I would be totally pleased with that. Isn't that the final goal? I took in another deep breath, my brain got quiet and I thought again,

"I've been good... I will eventually and ultimately be going to heaven, wouldn't I?"

The silence was overwhelming... not a soul, my soul, my higher self, my God would not even hint to me the answer.

Why wasn't anything satisfying anymore? Again, thinking back to when I was a kid, anything and everything was possible. I was highly motivated and unstoppable. I was happy. I was inspired. What happened? Why now, after all this time, was I SO BLAH? What happened in my past that manifested this transition of "WOW" to "YUCK"? How did I go from MOTIVATED to PROCRASTINATION and how can I get that MOTIVATION and PASSION back?

I was not a very religious person; spiritual, yes. Belief in God, yes. Higher self, spirits, signs, sure. I just laid in bed that day, contemplating my life and feeling distraught.

That evening came quickly. Still in bed, I prayed for something... Anything... A sign... A book... An email... A phone call... Anything to inspire me and give me just a tad of motivation (aside from having to get up to go to the bathroom) that would excite me to not only get up and provide a substantial reason to get out of bed, but also to continue on with my daily life, and give me back my sense of purpose and passion, even if it was only one step at a time...

Off to my amazing dreamland I drifted... deeper, and deeper into my subconscious mind to where all of my dreams and passions were alive and thriving.

Then, it came! One morning in my search for inspiration, I discovered the missing link that caused everything to change.

It wasn't enough for me to just ask and pray. I needed to take action in order to heal. I became passionate and inspired to share, and give back to the world!

For now, this is my "WHY"! I have to share with the world what I learned, what made a difference to me, and what you, too, can do if you are about to hit rock bottom.

The missing link (the one I mentioned earlier) that I'm going to share with you is how I learned to live a value

If you believe it will work out, You'll see opportunities. If you believe it won't, you will see obstacles.
~ Wayne dyer

driven and inspired life. How I let go and got out of a dead end relationship. I moved to the location of my favorite dream, and put myself in a position of freedom, (my number one life value) where every day I began to feel more and more fulfilled. This feeling of purpose and fulfillment became my motivation to not only write this book, but to also help other people overcome their own personal baggage and guide them towards self empowerment. I not only continue to give hope and inspiration daily to others, but prove to myself over and over again, that every day, anything in life can become possible... again!

In this book I will provide you with some heartwarming and heart-wrenching stories (my stories), along with introducing you to proven tools that work, and guide you on WHERE to go and WHO can you turn to, to help find and realign your passions. I will give you insights on HOW to clear your blocks, and additional education as to WHY you need to remove your negative emotions and limiting beliefs BEFORE you can truly allow yourself to live the life you have always dreamed about and desired.

However, these stories of my past disappointments, unforeseen circumstances, and shattered dreams really and truly don't matter. Everyone has their own story, some better, some worse, and some much more intense... the details just don't matter. Any psychiatrist and/or therapist that asks you to tell them your story and you end up associating yourself within those negative experiences may not be helping you as much as they could. I think of therapists like diets... they don't work the same for everyone. Some are good, some are great, and some just don't work. Since we are all wired similarly, although each of us is individually different based on upbringing, education, environment, and personal experiences, this timeline[4] therapy I'm about to share with you may also become your favorite approach to inner happiness and peace.

With MER® (Mental and Emotional Release), the Master Practitioner doesn't need to know the details, or even want to know the specifics of your story. The minute your Master Practitioner starts to believe your view of the world, they can no longer help you. The goal is to disassociate the feelings and emotions from the events that had occurred in the past. While figuring out how to reframe current thoughts and to dig deep to find the root cause of an unwanted problem. NLP (Neuro Linguistic Programming) gives us the tools to change perspectives and move from a world of impossibility into a world of possibility.

Although I'm going to share with you my stories, you can replace any of the Betrayal, Loss, Lies, Trauma, Anger, Sadness, Fear with stories from your own life. My life stories are to show you that you aren't alone, and how I, Liana (a nobody to those who have never met me) could let go of my past, get rid of the apathy, negativity,

I wish you Love. Love is the greatest healer. I hope it wells up within you, overflowing into the lives of others. May love always be with you.

and being stuck.

I was living in a world of people telling me to "just let it go and move on," with me not having a clue on HOW to "just let it go and move on." After years of counseling with numerous therapists, reading all the 'self-help' books, listening to motivational gurus sell me items from the stage, my research and training finally paid off. I finally learned the necessary tools and techniques that actually work. I want to scream out loud and share them with the world. So, with what I am going to share with you in this book, you can finally learn how to "just let it go and move on," too!

Perhaps it isn't until now, that anyone has guided you to WHERE to go, WHAT to do, and WHO can really help you overcome your past. Here are my stories and how I came to live the life I had always dreamed of living. And I'll provide you an abundance of resources to help you take the next step to become empowered and live the life you have always wanted to live!

My goal is to provide value to others, inspire, and through the process of MER®, guide other people in overcoming their mental stuckness, remove unhelpful and undesirable negative emotions as a result from their past life experiences, eliminate limiting beliefs, and live the purposeful, passionate life about which they have always dreamed.

Chapter 01

~ It's All Possible~

A s a kid, I thought everything was possible, even as a teenager and young adult... when others thought I should give up or not get my hopes up, I had the "I CAN do it" attitude and things generally worked themselves out. When I was a kid in junior high school, I received a letter in the mail. An invitation to try out for the 1984 Olympic Opening Ceremony's dance team. Just about ALL the Southern California girls ages 13-15 were invited to try out. There would be three levels of auditions over the next few months, and they would be narrowed down to best of the best and those special selected girls would have the opportunity to perform in front of the world.

I come from a family of dancers. My grandmother and a few of her sisters were Vaudeville dancers and entertainers. My mom had put my sister and I in dance, tap, ballet, and jazz classes for as long as I can remember. I was a Jr. High School cheerleader and I was really excited about this amazing opportunity.

My girlfriends and I would stretch every day to increase

our flexibility and made big plans to drive to the auditions together. Thousands and thousands of girls arrived at the stadium in the hopes that they too, would become an Olympic opening ceremony dancer. The Olympic Committee broke everyone down into groups, times, numbers, sections. We each joined our group, learned a basic routine and had just about 15 minutes to practice it before they would call our group in to be tested. I was surprised how quickly it went. A few counts of eight, a grapevine, a kick with each leg, a turn to the left, a turn to the right, a spin, a few cheerleader hand motions and we were done.

"Thank you," said the judges. "Check your mailboxes. You will hear back from us soon."

What were they looking for? How could they tell if we could dance from those few simple steps?

Anxiously I would run to the mailbox every day in the hopes that the next invitation would arrive. My parents and the other neighborhood parents would get together outside and talk in front of the house while we played in the streets; they were talking about how unlikely it would be for anyone they knew, any of their friends' kids to actually get chosen and would continually comment making sure none of us would get our hopes up.

A few days later a friend called me, she said that she didn't make it but it was cool, she didn't want to waste her entire summer practicing anyway, she would rather go to the beach, movies, mall, and hang out with all of our friends at the pool. I was surprised because I thought she was a really good dancer. We took classes together and if anyone was able to do it, I thought it would be her. Days went by, and I still didn't get my rejection letter. Finally, with hope still in my mind, I ran to the mailbox as I had done every day since the first audition and there it was, the letter addressed to me, postmarked from the Olympic committee. I ran back into the house, into the kitchen where Mom was cooking dinner...

"It's Here! It's Here"!

"Did you open it?" she asked.

"Not yet. I wanted to do it with you when I read that I'm going to the next audition."

"Now, Liana, you know there were a lot of very good professional dancers at the audition, I wouldn't be too disappointed if it doesn't happen. I'm here for you."

Ignoring her lack of encouragement, I ripped open the letter, unfolded it and started to read...

Dear Liana... Congratulations!

"WooHoo!" I screamed, "I'm going to the next audition."

My mom, with a funky grunt face smile, congratulated me, hugged me and exclaimed, "WOW! That's terrific!"

I don't think it quite hit her as she still looked a bit

You as much as anyone in the universe deserve your love and respect. ~ Buddha confused or in disbelief. I was so happy, I noticed her funny expression, tried to ignore it and just ran off to call my friends.

Mom drove me to the next audition, it was very similar but much less people. Hundreds and hundreds of girls, if not thousands were already eliminated and didn't make the cut. This time the routine was a little more complicated, but not by much. Maybe a full minute routine, not even enough moves to complete an entire song.

Same thing, 15 minutes of rehearsal and we were on stage in front of the judges. Before I knew it, "Thank you... Don't forget to check your mailboxes." And we all left crossing our fingers that we would be invited to move on.

Back and forth to the mailbox I ran. More and more friends were cut and at this point everyone I knew was kind of over it. They were making plans for the summer, pool parties scheduled, Magic Mountain, Disneyland... all the fun summer events we looked forward to doing together. Finally, another letter arrived and I ran in to the kitchen again with Mom, where she tried to assure me that she would be proud of me no matter what... even if I didn't get to the next level. I slowly opened the envelope with the Olympic Committee stamp on the front, closed my eyes, and prayed silently in my own mind, "Please, God, let me dance at the Olympics..."

Dear Liana... Congratulations!!!

"YES!" I screamed. "I made the final round."

I was SO excited I wanted to scream it to the entire world. Instead, I just called my dad at work.

"Way to Go!" he encouraged. "I knew you could do it! That's my Girl!"

When I hung up with Dad, I called another friend who at this point couldn't care less and wasn't very supportive. Busy confirming her other summer plans, she suggested I should skip the last audition and come to the pool party that was scheduled on the same day. She said, "Come to the party, you're probably not going to make the team anyway... Why bother?"

Alright... have you ever heard the expression, "Don't pee in my Cheerios?" Well, DANG! My box of Cheerios was already rotten before I poured them into the bowl. There was SO much negative talk from my friends about how it was most likely rigged or the rich kids' parents probably bought off the committee members. They said I could never be that good and asked, why would the judges choose me? Definitely not to get my hopes up, because there were SO MANY BETTER DANCERS out there than me. We didn't know anyone from my school who had made it to the third round. My mom's way to encourage me was to continually reminding me that she would still be proud of me no matter what... EVEN... not

IF, but WHEN I didn't make it. It was great that I made it THIS far.

Why at this time in my life did I choose not to listen? I didn't care, I ignored everyone's negative comments and deep down in my heart I knew I was meant to dance for the opening ceremonies. I showed up at the final audition and actually recognized one other girl who was a fellow cheerleader. She recognized me, too. She ran across the room to say hello. We hugged and congratulated each other for making it this far. She whispered in my ear that her mother overheard some of the judges talking, and they stated that almost all of the positions were full, there was just enough room for only a handful more. There were still over a hundred girls standing around and we were in the very last group. We were soon called into the practice room to learn the final steps of the last routine and my heart sank. I looked around at all the tall, blonde, lengthy, flexible, talented girls stretching in their cute leotards, Flash Dance, off the shoulder t-shirts, and I started to doubt myself.

Could I really do this? Should I keep trying to do this? Should I have gone to the fun pool party that I'm missing with all my other friends?

How would you feel? Think about it for a minute... Standing there in a group of models and beauties, who have been dancing probably since birth... then there was me, short, brunette, stocky, with everyone telling me that

This above all, to thine own self be true. ~ William Shakespeare

I'm not that good and not to get my hopes up... 5,6,7,8... I took a deep breath in and went through the last practice round and then grabbed my towel to wipe off the pool of sweat. The Main Olympic Coordinator came to the front of the room and made an announcement.

"Okay, Ladies, this is it! Thank you all for coming... We are going to line everyone up in rows and I want you all to keep dancing until the music stops. All the girls who get tapped on the shoulder should immediately go to the back table and write on the backside of your large audition number, your name and phone number and make sure you leave it with the representative at the back table... while (he took a big deep breath) everyone who wasn't chosen, please stay in your spot, out of the way... Be patient and just wait for those who have been picked to collect their things and coordinate where to go next."

My heart started to pound while my mind began to wander; no more practice time... are my kicks ready? Will I remember my steps? Would I be in the final handful, chosen to be a dancer in the 1984 Olympic Opening Ceremonies?

My heart pounded harder and harder. I started to sweat again when I heard the music starting to play... I could barely hear the music, I could barely breathe... my heart was pounding just as loud if not louder than the music... then all of a sudden, I was able to

Life is short, break the rules, forgive quickly, kiss slowly, love truly, laugh uncontrollably and never regret anything makes you smile. ~ Mark Twain *focus, I tuned into the instructor as he called out the numbers, "5,6,7,8" and I began to dance...*

I danced like I had never danced before. Smiled from ear to ear, toes pointed, kicks high, arms strong. I could see the judges walking up and down the aisles looking for personality, energy, smiles, talent.

This was the last time in my life I distinctly remember feeling like It's All Possible.

Chapter 02

~ Betrayal~

It reminds me of another summer afternoon I try hard not to think about... Just as I squinted into the bright, warm, setting sun, I parked the car on the side of the driveway and headed towards the front door.

It was just like any ordinary late afternoon in summer, the days were hot and the sun didn't set until really late. I was just a few months over 16 years and I was able take the car to drive around the valley to visit my grandma, go out with friends, and of course help Mom with her errands. The main thing I was responsible for was taking my little sister to dance class.

She was an amazing dancer. She started at age three in a little yellow leotard and tights. It was her passion, she wanted to be a dancer probably before she could walk, she watched "The Nutcracker" on TV and decided that she was going to be Clara. She didn't really seem to care about anything else except becoming a prima ballerina and would joke about living alone like a hermit in a dark cave. She hated the sun and for some reason her car seat seemed to always be in the direct sunlight. Right now her cave was her bedroom where she would keep the shutters closed and play with her paper dolls for hours. She was quiet and generally kept to herself.

She in a sense was also very mature for her age. Although in my eyes, she screamed from the day she was born until what seemed like forever. I can remember hearing that noise continuing all the way through the halls during all hours of the day and night. Mom said she wanted to run before she could crawl, eat by herself before she had teeth and do things for herself before she could even hold a spoon. She definitely wanted to talk as soon as she came out of the womb. She continued to scream until the day she could actually talk... it was just this loud bellowing guttural howl that came out. She was always red in the face, until the day she started verbally saying letters, talking, and putting sentences together which pretty much happened all in the same week.

Once grown up, she commented that she didn't like people talking or screaming at each other or at her. She told me later in life that she, as a kid, thought that life around her was on sensory overload. She didn't want to be center of attention. I know I would become so frustrated when she wouldn't shut up, I was probably the one screaming at her which would just make her scream

I never saw a wild thing sorry for itself. A small bird will drop frozen dead from a bough without ever having felt sorry for itself. ~ D.H. Lawrence louder. She stated later in life that she felt everything and everyone was always directly in her face. She wanted to be alone, in the quiet, calm, dark space, perhaps with some soft classical music to self sooth and escape the chaos of life's daily interactions.

Most of the time, if I was out, Mom wanted me home by the time the street lights turned on. I had a job at our local temple tutoring kids that were learning Hebrew and preparing them to become a bar/bat mitzvah. That's the coming of age when a kid would be accepted in the Jewish community as an adult. I remember this one late afternoon, after coming home from a good day at work, walking in the front door to our house, the door closed behind me and I was able to see the sharp, brightly saturated, striped lights of a thin rainbow alongside the wall. It only happened at a very particular time of the day when the sun was getting ready to set behind the hill across the street from our house. The sun found and shined its way through the tiny peephole in the front door, casting the different colored rays of light all the way down the long hallway across each of the many picture frames and continued past the hallway light switch across the perpendicular hall until it disappeared around the corner.

I gradually walked down the long hallway entrance following this thin rainbow light with the tip of my finger, trailing it up and down, across the bumpy fabric patterned wallpaper keeping a close watch on each color

In the confrontation between the stream and the rock, the stream always wins - not through strength, but through persistence. ~ Buddha until I reached the end where it gradually disappeared. I dropped my jacket on the barstool and hollered out, "Hi! I'm home!"

Silence filled the air... Mom and Dad turned off the TV and stepped around the far corner barstools to greet me with sad faces. I knew something was wrong. "Is it Grandma?" I asked.

"No."

"My little dog?" I questioned.

"No," Dad quietly replied again.

"What's wrong?" I asked.

"It's Chrissy." Then there was a long pause... My mind was a little confused. Chrissy was my cousin. Fun and young, either in her late 20s or very early 30s. She was like a best friend or super fun big sister to me... I couldn't even imagine anything that would be wrong. I was excited with anticipation and continually thinking about what activities we would be doing together since I knew we would be able to hang out together as my summer break was approaching. I spent part of each of my school vacations with her. "Am I still going out to see her or is she going out of town?" I asked.

"Chrissy," he whispered as if he couldn't even get the words out any louder... "She's gone. She was killed in a car accident." He took in several small breaths prior to a big deep breath. And with eyes swollen and tears dripping down his cheek, he sniffled while releasing the words, "And hit by a big semi truck."

My mouth dropped open and my heart sunk. Chrissy treated me like she really cared. She was a cousin by marriage, and had two sons who were like my little brothers. I spent every school holiday that I was allowed to at their house in Rialto, California. We swam in their pool, we went out shopping, baked in her kitchen, stopped at cute little outside cafés or restaurants to try new foods and enjoyed spending time with her boys.

The boys were young, one was just a toddler, the cutest little thing. I used to hold him, humming little songs and walking around the house with him in my arms until he fell asleep. I was able to change his diaper, and watch him coo and play with the plastic ice popsicles that he loved to chew on during his teething phase. Jeff, her older son, from what I remember I think he was six or seven, Chrissy's son from her first marriage, was like a cool little brother. He was very well mannered and private like my sister was at home. He sort of stuck to himself, was very soft spoken, and played quietly with his neighborhood friends. I felt very protective of him, I wanted to make sure that his voice was always heard and his opinions considered. I know he was a bit timid and I imagined that if anyone was to bully him around at school... they would have to stand up to me! For some reason I felt I needed to take on the role of his big sister

If you have built castles in the air, your work need not be lost; That is where they should be. Now put foundations under them. ~ Henry David Thoreau and make sure he was always taken care of.

It was always an enjoyable, easygoing carefree time, hide and seek in the streets, baseball in the yard, iced tea by the pitcher. Life was great as a kid whenever I could visit and stay with Chrissy and her family. We would hang out in the kitchen and make lasagna, or bake cookies. Her house always smelled so inviting. As you walked in the front door of their home there was this beautiful, colorful Calder mobile that would always catch my attention as the slight breeze from the opening and shutting of the front door would brush across each perfect shape, sending all of them into motion like a beautiful hypnotic dance of colors inviting me into my next magical adventure. We continually had a great time. In fact, I cannot remember not having some wonderful story to tell my friends about my amazing vacation with cousin Chrissy.

Over the next few seconds, while still standing numb in the hallway, I slowly slid down the fabric covered wall and ended up sitting on the old golden carpet, as my mind continued to wander. I didn't know how to react, I didn't know how to process what was just said... I just was thinking how being at Chrissy's house wasn't anything like my house. My mind started churning and all types of visions and thoughts started pouring into my head. Chrissy's house was calm, not chaotic like mine, where Mom and Dad would fight about silly things.

You can't start the next chapter of your life if you keep re-reading the last one.

I felt that my parents' way of communicating was by screaming across the house. They would pick fights with each other, slam doors and then my sister and I would either go hide in my room, or as I got older, I would play referee. When the screaming finally subsided, me and my sister would come out of our bedrooms to check things out, their bedroom door would be locked and they had a rule, "Don't knock or bother Mommy and Daddy when the door is locked. Just stay quiet and keep busy." So, we would lay on the carpet together outside their door and flip through some of the books in the tall bookshelf just outside their bedroom door. Not understanding until much later in life, that was their ritual for "make up sex".

Once my little sister was old enough to talk, she was very antisocial, at least with me. She loved to sit by herself in her room and play with her paper dolls. She would cut them out, create her own outfits out of toilet paper, construction paper, pretty much anything she could create. If not a famous ballerina, I thought she might grow up to be a fashion designer. Although her taste in her own clothing could use some help, she tended to dress very plain with no style, oversized t-shirts, never any jewelry or make up, and didn't really care what the other kids were wearing. In fact, I think she got great pleasure out of showing off the next odd outfit she found shopping at the thrift store. In high school, she dyed her hair and dressed up Goth. My friends and I thought

If you are a going through hell, keep going. ~ Winston Churchill

she was weird. Although weird, I knew that one day she would blossom and turn into something absolutely amazing! Whether it was as a ballerina in a professional company, a famous fashion designer, or a president of a corporation, she was disciplined and very, very smart.

My sister loved to read. She would occasionally pick up one of those huge encyclopedias from the bookshelf and read it to me while we waited for Mom and Dad to finish behind their locked door. Sometimes I would have her read to me my homework assignments, especially if they were long books. I had no interest in reading anything except the "Cliff's notes". One or two paragraphs I would read and reread, looking up all the unfamiliar words that I didn't understand and quickly become exhausted trying to comprehend all the random information that in my mind was meaningless and didn't make any sense. I would simply close my eyes and since I was so tired I would just fall asleep.

Dreaming was my escape. Dreaming was one of the few things I enjoyed to do by myself. I always needed to be with people and never felt comfortable doing things on my own. Although independent and able to accomplish anything in my dream world, I tended to struggle with friends and being part of the cool group in school. Later in life, I learned that I was an auditory learner with additional learning disabilities. No one would ever know, how would they? Since my sister loved to read, she would read to me my junior high and high school books when she was just 7 or 8. Did I mention that she was five years younger than me? In fact, she was so smart, she would even proofread my term papers if Mom and Dad were busy. I had my way of compensating and getting by. I remember that I really wanted a sister, and when she was born, although she screamed as a baby and tended to spend time alone in her room, I wanted us to be close. I knew that if I could convince her to help me, our bond might grow, and as much as she wanted to be a loner, she was too smart and helpful to be left alone.

Ultimately, she must have gotten her fashion sense from my mom who definitely was not the fashion queen either. She would say, "If you want those name brand jeans then you have to go to work and pay to buy them yourself." And, "If you want a phone in your room, go get a job so you can pay the bill." She was surprised when I came from temple at age 12 and a half with a good paying job. I came to the conclusion at a young age and made the decision that her comments were meant to discourage me. She didn't think I could get a job so in her own way, instead of saying no, she came up with a reason why I couldn't.

Unfortunately, like many teenage girls and their mothers, we fought a lot as I was growing up. Dad would take my side, I would take his, and my mom would pout and play the victim role, and I would end up being the bitch who would sarcastically make mean comments and rub it in. It was my way to cope with my feelings of insecurity and

Don't downgrade your dream just to fit your reality. Upgrade your conviction to match your destiny.

how I thought I could never be good enough for her. There was a lot of tension between me and Mom. I think I really tried to prove her wrong most of the time. Which may have been her original intent to motivate me. If she said I couldn't do something, I would find a way. If she said I couldn't get or have something, I'd find a way. From getting a job at 12, to buying designer pants at 14 and buying a boat after college because I wanted to learn how to water ski. Mom always thought there was a better way to act, to do it, or to spend my money. I felt that I constantly disappointed her and that may have been one of the reasons I felt that she continued to put me at the bottom of her priority list.

After me, Mom tried to have more kids. She had some kind of problem where she had to carry her dead babies in her belly to the full term. So, for many of those years she stayed in bed and was not only exhausted, but seemed very sad and depressed. After the two miscarriages my parents started talking about adoption. I always thought Mom wanted another kid because I wasn't what she was hoping for, or for some reason I wasn't and never felt good enough. She repeatedly said that my grandfather wanted a boy and gave her a hard time about me being a girl. She kept pushing me away and onto my dad. Not sure if it was my looks, my personality, my hyper activity, or what that just made Mom want something more or someone different than me. She never seemed happy with me. Mom and I had

Definiteness of purpose is the starting point of all achievement. ~ W. Clement Stone an odd, distant relationship growing up. As a kid, I thought she didn't like me very much. She would come home from work and ignore me, stating she needed her downtime. "Don't talk to me for at least an hour after I get home," she would yell. "I've been around kids all day and I just don't want to hear it," she would scream. Then she would go off to the kitchen or read the newspaper. When we did interact, she would generally give me the dissatisfied look and roll her eyes at me. Like I was doing something or saying something wrong. She would constantly tell me to sit still. I didn't know what to do to make her proud of me. Over the years, my mom was the one to set my limits and create my boundaries. Dad used to joke around and call Mom a prude. Mom insisted on teaching me about not having sex until marriage, and tried to raise me "right" with the same good old fashioned values. I guess it worked.

I was pretty naive for a 16 year old. Although I had several boyfriends, we never got past first or second base. I guess you could call me a late bloomer. I enjoyed the company of boys and preferred hanging out with them compared to girls probably because I was pretty much a tomboy. Even through college most of my friends were boys. I enjoyed playing hide and seek in the street and kickball with the neighborhood boys. I enjoyed being around and could relate better to boys. Girls seemed to be a little too prissy or mellow for my outgoing, never sit still personality. Although being friends with mostly

When what you are doing is an expression of your purpose, it often doesn't feel like work at all.
~ Dr. Matt James

boys, I didn't end up having sex until a few years into college. And that was a major family ordeal. I was home for summer break and had a steady boyfriend. There was an ongoing family joke that seemed to go on for months, every time I would talk to my mom on the phone she would ask, "Are you still my little girl?" She would ask in such a way that it seemed, if I didn't answer, "Yes, Mom, I'm still your little girl," she would be disappointed and have no more respect for me. For weeks at the dinner table, where the family always had our time together, we were all free to express our opinions and talk about anything and everything. I was discouraged from "doing it" and it was discussed out in the open... usually at the dinner table, if I did decide to do it, they instigated discussions of what to expect for the first time.

Yes. It got crazy. From laughter, to tears, to screaming, to sarcastic insults. That is the specific location where I learned how communication worked best for me. I was able to "handle" and "end" the uncomfortable situations that transpired at the dinner table. I felt like I needed to deal with my mom and her condescending attitude and a quick fix to stop my parents from bickering. I finally came to the conclusion that the only way to get through dinnertime was to become a sarcastic bitch.

So, when Mom would say something like, "I don't think you should..." I would rudely interrupt her with a sarcastic comment, "Ah, you didn't think I could... did you? Well, I can, and I did!"

And then, finally it came. The evening of "my first time." It happened at my parents' house when they went out of town for the weekend. Of course, I got the call later that evening... "Are you still my little girl?'" was the first question out of her mouth.

"No, Mom," I interrupted... "I'm your big girl now!"

When Mom and Dad were arguing about stuff, anything at all, I would just end the argument by sarcastically blurting out, "OH, poor me! I'm the victim, everyone is picking on me." Then Mom would get up, walk away, and the fighting and yelling at each other across the table was quickly put to an end.

Finally, the deed was done, and my mission accomplished. I could just sit and eat my dinner.

Mom was thrifty. Generally a discount store shopper, having grown up in Los Angeles with her mother, father, sister, aunt, uncle, and cousin, my dad used to joke about all they would give her was a hot turkey sandwich from the Thrifty's Drug store.

Not that me and my sister were in need of anything extra, but, Chrissy, who I was just beside myself with disbelief was now gone, would spend the afternoon going to chic boutiques and high end department stores. She would pick out the most awesome outfit and have me try it on. She made me feel like something so special, I loved her and her family SO much. I prayed that

If you cant figure out your purpose, figure out your passion. For your passion will lead you directly to your purpose.

someday I would grow into such a wonderful person and be able to share similar great times with my future nieces or nephews, too.

Thinking back to the summer before high school, we spent several long weekends, three straight days each, coming up with the best cheerleading tryout routine ever. She helped me with rhyming words, the moves, the jumps... We practiced over and over again until it was perfect. We both were confident that when tryouts were scheduled, there was no way I wouldn't make the squad. Chrissy was the best! Always putting a smile on everyone's face. I quickly took in a deep breath after those few seconds of thought...

Oh my Gosh! She's dead. What am I going to do? This is the most horrible thing that could ever happen. What about the boys? What about her husband? What are they going to do without her?

She was the glue that made that family so amazing. She cooked, cleaned, cheered everyone on, supported their needs and made everyone happy.

I couldn't believe it... she was gone.

The hallway was silent, another few seconds passed and it felt like hours. No one knew what to say. Dad came over and gave me a big hug. He didn't know all the details, but said he would tell me as soon as he found out from Rick, his cousin, Chrissy's husband. I was numb and the tears wouldn't stop dripping down my cheeks. How could I express to those young boys that I would always be there for them just as their mother was always there for me. I decided to write them a little note. The little note turned into a three page letter that went on and on about how sorry I was for their loss and how at this particular moment I promised, even swore on their mother's grave, that I would be there for anything they ever needed, I wouldn't let them down and they could always count on me.

My favorite memories were with them and their mom, and I would do anything to bring her back if I could, and I still wanted to be a big part of their lives. As the tears dripped onto the page, I could write no more. No more words would be able to express the sadness in my heart and the promise that I made not only to myself, and Chrissy, but also to those boys.

By this time it was dark and turning into night. I wanted to drive out to Rialto, to be there for the boys, I couldn't imagine they were just home acting as normal getting ready for bed... Mom said it was too late, and I could go in the morning. I knew they would need food, comfort, hugs... I knew I needed some.

The next morning I was up and ready early, I packed my overnight bag just in case I could be helpful over there and if Rick needed me to watch the kids while he took

The best day of your life is the one on which you decide your life is your own. No apologies or excuses. No one to lean on, rely on, or blame. You alone are responsible for the quality of it. ~ Bob Moawad care of any necessary logistics. Rick was a cool guy. A private investigator. Always dressed well and smelled of cologne. I admired him since one day I wanted to be an undercover cop, I thought he would maybe one day be able to teach me how to shoot a gun. He drove a cool sports car, not the one I would choose, but it was hot and it could drive fast.

I remember a week when I was out there visiting, just after I got my driver's permit, he said that it was important to learn how to drive a stick shift car. We never had one in our house and I had no idea what to do. Rick explained it all step by step... sat in the passenger seat, set his gun in the center console, and said in his strong authoritative voice, "If you stall it, I'll shoot you!"

"What?"

I kind of laughed under my breath and was also slightly terrified at the same time.

In today's world, having an adult with a loaded gun sitting next to the driver would have been a total 'Red Flag'. But, in the 80s it was not out of the ordinary and similar to hitchhiking, riding in the back of a pickup truck or not wearing a seatbelt. So, it did not cause much, if any, need for alarm.

I did exactly what he had told me and sure enough, within about four minutes I was speeding down the open road in his black Porsche. Didn't stall it once... until we got back in the driveway and I took my foot off the clutch. Oops. At least it wasn't going onto the freeway on ramp. Very cool! My first lesson and now I can drive a stick shift and have a story to tell all about it. I learned on a sports car! A sporty black Porsche to be exact.

I arrived at my cousin's house expecting it to be a somber morning. But, to my surprise, the boys were all playing outside in the pool. I gave the usual hugs and hellos, and for a moment I thought I was in a dream. It was very surreal, nothing seemed out of place. There were a few dishes left in the sink, and toys on the floor, but overall it seemed pretty normal. Rick said, in his generally authoritative voice, "Go grab a soda and come out to the pool." I went upstairs to put my stuff down and change into my bathing suit just as Jeff was just heading inside to go change into his street clothes since he had plans to head over to his friend's house. He said, "Hi, and see you later" and that he would be back in a couple of hours. Dov, the youngest, following close behind went upstairs to play with his toys in his room. I changed, grabbed my soda and went back downstairs and outside to the pool.

Now this is when everything got a little weird. Rick was now on the phone sunbathing in the nude. I looked over at him and apprehensively asked, "Did you lose something?"

"No, I don't want tan lines, you can take yours off too."

"I'm good thanks," I said as I jumped into the pool. I

Sometimes "Home" is not a Place... It's a Person.

found an inner tube and lay comfortably inside with my toes splashing in the cool water. I faced the back side of the pool, so I didn't need to look at him lying there tanning.

Within 15 minutes his good friend and neighbor from down the street came over. With a bottle of wine in hand, he closed the slider door, refilled Rick's cup, set the bottle down on the little side table under the tan umbrella and jumped, splashing me, into the pool. After a few more swigs, Rick jumped in with a big cannonball splash, too. A little playful splashing and squirting with the kids' water guns and things were off to a fairly odd, yet, playful morning.

The fun and laughter must have intrigued Dov because he came running downstairs wanting to join the party. Rick told him to get back upstairs and go to his room, explaining he did something earlier to get into trouble and needed to stay upstairs.

"I'm hungry", Dov replied. "I want something to eat."

So, I asked Rick what I could go make for him?

"He is fine," he insisted. "Just go upstairs, we will be inside for lunch in a few minutes."

As Dov turned around to go upstairs, Rick untied my bikini top and pulled it off.

"Hey, give that back!" I shouted out, totally embarrassed

The older you get, the more you realize... you have no desire for drama or conflict. You just want a cozy home, a good book, and a person who knows how you like your coffee.

as I covered up my teenage breasts.

"You want it, come and get it," he said in a playful tone.

As I reached for it, he threw it over to his friend and then he grabbed me by the waist. He pulled me close then started to bounce me up and down on his now extremely hard package. With one hand he was trying to pull my bottoms off and penetrate me through the side, and with his other arm wrapped around my body gripping both my hands together so I couldn't escape. Squeezing me tighter and tighter, bouncing me harder up and down on his lap, as I kicked and struggled. His grip got stronger and stronger and he became much more forceful as his friend swam closer. He threw me over to his friend who grabbed me by the neck in a choke hold trying to do the same thing. Rick swam over and groped my breasts while his friend started pulling down my bathing suit bottoms. I managed to flail around enough to escape the choke hold and kick Rick in the gut hard enough to push away allowing me to swim to the side of the pool. I hopped out of the pool without my top and while looking back, headed across the yard to go inside the house and get to safety. As I looked over my shoulder, right behind me was Rick in all his nakedness and hard on already starting to chase me into the house. He yelled, "Get back here!" as I started to run toward the screen patio door. I dripped water through the house, almost slipping. I managed to get about 1/3 of the way up the stairs when Rick grabbed my leg and pulled me

5 Rules to live a happier life: 1) love yourself 2) Do good 3) Always forgive 4) Harm no one 5) Be positive

back down causing a painful rug burn down my thigh all the way to the side of my knee. He turned me over and ripped off my bikini bottoms with one hand and with the other roughly clinching my arms together above my head. As I kicked and squirmed around in disbelief I started screaming. Who knew what would happen next?

I feel the weight of his hot, sweaty chest pushing against my neck and ear. The water keeps dripping into my eyes from his hair and face. I close my eyes as I feel his hard dick push its way in between my thighs. Wiggling and squirming I keep screaming for him to stop!

He was just laughing as his grip became tighter and his demeanor became less playful and much more forceful. "Please stop!" I yelled as tears started to flow and I knew I was in trouble, I just wanted to leave. I screamed out at the top of my lungs, "HELP!"

The only one around in the house was little Dov, who magically appeared at the top of the stairs and asked if it was now time to eat?

"God Dammit!" Rick yelled as he looked up. "Get back into your room!"

Dov turned around and stormed off, all I could hear after his door slammed shut was the heavy heartbeats and wrestling sounds of two wet naked bodies.

Shit!... downstairs at the sliding glass door, now stood his friend peeking in, also naked; Rick had somehow automatically locked the door and his friend could not get in. As Rick continued to hold me down, I think the thrill of his friend joining in must have made him more excited. So, as I kicked and struggled, I managed to free myself (or he miraculously just let me go) as he popped up and jumped down the few stairs to unlock the sliding door for his friend. Not knowing what else to do, I pulled myself up, ran the rest of the way upstairs and locked myself into the bedroom with Dov.

As Rick banged and pounded on the door that I now sat against, curled up behind... With tears in my eyes, dripping down my cheeks, I whispered to Dov, "Everything is going to be okay, I'm gonna be okay, I'm here for you, I always will be."

He smiled his little toddler smile and continued to play with his toys. I guess Rick figured that I would have to eventually leave the room, so both men quietly went downstairs to get another drink.

The moment I heard the slider open, I quickly stepped out, grabbed my bag, threw on shorts and a tank top, put the letter I wrote to the boys on Jeff's bed, and as fast as I could, ran down the stairs, out the front door, into my car and headed straight home. The tears wouldn't stop pouring down my face.

What the heck just happened? Should I have

Everything we hear is an opinion, not a fact. Everything we see is a perspective not the truth - Marcus Aurelius *taken Dov with me? Should I go back and get him? I don't want to go back there. I never want to see Rick again. Thoughts were racing through my mind. Are the boys going to be in trouble? What is going to happen to them?*

What could I do? I felt dirty, my shorts were wet because I never had time to dry off, I was sweaty from the summer heat and just threw on the first thing I saw inside on top of my bag. My heart was pounding with disbelief. Tears filled my eyes so I could barely see. I trusted Rick like family, like a brother... this was Chrissy's husband... and she JUST DIED!

Is he insane? Did I provoke it? All I wanted to do was be there for them, like they were always there for me. I cried all the way home and didn't want to tell a soul. I was raised to be open and communicate, that it's best not to let things fester inside, but, I was SO embarrassed. Two grown men had seen my boobs, there was a hard penis shoved between my legs. It was new, it was scary and disturbing, my heart was still beating heavily, I was so confused. I didn't know what to do.

What do I do? How do I act? I'm agitated and restless... But, thank God nothing actually happened... Thank you, God!

There was nothing that could be done. No proof of anything, it would be his word against mine. Would

Overthinking = The art of creating problems that don't exist.
Overthinking leads to negative thoughts...Stop overthinking.

Mom blame me? After a few days of shock and numbness over Chrissy's death, I'm pretty sure I was still acting a bit out of sorts. Much quieter than usual, keeping to myself and staying alone in my room. Mom must have noticed since she came into my room and asked if I wanted to talk. Of course, the tears started flowing and I told her what had happened. As I was getting into the details, she interrupted... "I'll kill him!" she exclaimed.

"No, Mom. Nothing happened, I'm OK. I'm just not comfortable going over there anymore."

Although I really wanted to be close and had every intention of always being there for the boys, I told my mom, "I just don't want to put myself in a position where I will ever see him again."

I didn't want my dad to know, I didn't want anyone to know. I was embarrassed, confused, and felt betrayed. I didn't want to dwell on it. Or even discuss it further. I was naive, unsure of myself and insecure with my body.

At that point in my life, although I may have let a boy allow his hand to crawl up my shirt, I certainly never had been naked or groped, or put in any type of situation like that. I just thought it would be best to forget it ever happened and not draw any attention to it. Not make a big deal about it. I felt even uncomfortable telling her about it and getting it off my chest.

At that time, Mom also relinquished that a long time ago when Rick and Chrissy were first married, Rick tried to hit on her one day in front of Dad in the jacuzzi, she didn't think much of it because Dad and Chrissy were both there... Anyway, she said nothing happened with them either. "Mom," I said, "let's just let it rest, I'm okay."

Life goes on. And it did.

As I think back to that day... even right now, it reminds me of a story I heard about how similar we are to the crab. Most animals, when caught need to be put into a cage or covered up to prevent them from escaping... not the crab. It is in their nature to prevent the other crabs from accomplishing what they want. As one crab will try to crawl out of its bucket, another crab will reach up and pull him down trying to free himself... It's one of the only animals that sabotages one another in hopes to either give themselves the upper hand or to bring others into their same unfortunate circumstance. I thought about it for a long time.

Why would my cousin, who I'm trying to help, betray me in such a way? Was he so upset he wanted to blame and take it out on someone? Did he want others who had nothing to do with his recent tragedy to suffer? Did he just want to show he had more control over me?

Is it a cultural or learned behavior, or is it instinctual, like the crab? What is the lesson I needed to learn? I sure

The best way to appreciate those you love is to think ahead and picture your life without them.

didn't know what it was, I just wanted to put the incident behind me and never think about it again.

You can never win an argument with a negative person. They only hear what suits them, and listen only to respond. ~ Michael P. Watson

Every challenge we face is sent by the universe
for only one reason;
For us to become
the best version of ourselves.

~ Kabbalah

Chapter 03

~Secrets & Decline~

My father had been battling lymphoma cancer for about seven years. He became diabetic, and needed regular insulin shots since he did not care to make smart choices regarding what he ate. He just wanted to enjoy his meals and eat with gusto... and he did. Like I mentioned earlier, dinner was family time and my family was crazy at the dinner table, we would take that time and communicate about anything and everything. Body parts, sex, vomit, gross things, funny things... I could make my mom pee in her pants as my ridiculous commentary got her laughing so hard. My sister and my dad would call us 'A house of vulgar barbarians'... and for some reason we were all proud of it.

Dad, over time, instead of eating with gusto, would nibble, cough, and choke regularly. We were all concerned. Weaker and weaker he became. During the days and weeks when I stayed to help out my mom, he became much weaker. He needed to stop and rest in between steps and it took us much longer to get out of the house when he had several doctor appointments and chemo treatments throughout the week. My dad had gone from looking like a young 50 year old to someone almost unrecognizable in a very short time.

In 2003, I became a foster mom. I had an amazing little boy who I took to soccer, T-ball, the park, and we loved to spend weekends with the grandparents... My parents. My little foster kid, let's call him Timmy, was the first grandchild. And proud grandparents they were. From science projects with Grandma and kicking the soccer ball through the field with Grandpa, these were what I would call our family's magical moments. Timmy and I would drive over two hours to visit my folks who at the time were living in the Valley (Yes, Oh MY GOD! I was raised a Valley Girl), which was becoming more and more of a hassle with our scheduled weekly visits to the local jail, therapist, and social services appointments.

Now, with Timmy's kindergarten quickly approaching and Dad just recently being diagnosed with the cancer, Dad decided to retire early and Mom had just a little under a year to go before they could travel and enjoy their retirement together. They were looking forward to their golden years of fun and travel. We started to look at some beautiful affordable properties near me in Orange County. With my true desire and intention to adopt Timmy, I hoped we could all share in the American dream and enjoy the closeness of our entire family by spending lots of fun times including all the holidays together gathered around Mom's dining room table.

We found some good doctors for Dad, and before you knew it, they were within a 15-20 minute commute of my Orange County condo. Ahh. We could all go out to dinner, they could attend Timmy's ball games, school performances, watch him if I got lucky enough to find a date, and best of all we could create more precious lasting memories.

Unfortunately, each time Dad went through his chemo treatments, he would end up getting very sick and weak. Pneumonia would set in and the doctors would have to sedate him so deeply that they insisted on putting him into medically induced comas. Mom and I would stay with him, hold his hand, Mom would stroke his hair and sit next to him for hours and hours. Every night before we would leave the hospital we would stand over his bed and pray, chant some healing blessings, time after time again. After a few days he would wake up with some crazy story about the nurse who wanted to take him away on vacation. He tried to convince us not to ever go back to the bad place... except he stated, "I just remembered, I need to go back and pick up my watch. I left my watch... the one with the red band, the wet red band."

We wondered what was going on in his subconscious mind that would cause those visions - the things he was hallucinating about and would remember as if they were so real and vivid, after being sedated and in a coma for three or four days.

Some people will have to learn how to appreciate you by losing you.

Along with all the stress of my father's illness causing many days off work and hospital visits, after three amazing years, I received a call from Social Services informing me that my dream to adopt Timmy would be put to an end. We needed to prepare my family and Timmy for heartbreak as my little boy, who I loved as my own, was to leave my world and be reunified with his biological father.

Fortunately, as timing happened to work out, Dad was just released from the hospital to give his only grandson a hug and kiss goodbye. Hoping and dreaming to either be reunited or have other grandkids to love and spoil.

Each time Dad would get released from the hospital he would, in my eyes, look as if he had aged about 10-15 years. His skin became thin and wrinkled, his hair thinning, falling out and becoming much more gray. He started moving more slowly, and getting so... so weak and tired.

Mom would call and tell me how she had to call the paramedic to help him get up because he fell over and no longer had the strength to climb the one stair that went from the garage to get him into the house. And, how he had fallen in the kitchen or bathroom and she wasn't strong enough to help him back up on her own. He eventually accepted the chore of carrying an oxygen tank around with him and tried to use a cane. He would just carry the cane up in the air and knock it into things as he walked by, it didn't do him much good. Soon he needed a walker to walk. That's when he decided that he didn't want to go out in public. He just wanted to stay in bed and we noticed how quickly he became very withdrawn and sad.

Then I introduced to him the mechanical carts in the supermarkets. He was nervous at first, but then he found his new mobile freedom and his will to live came back since he could now ride over to the deli department and try all the fresh samples of meats and cheeses. It was great to see him getting around and not feeling so sorry for himself. It was very sad watching my dad grow old and frail.

I still imagined him walking me down the aisle... first skipping, then walking, then I thought, maybe with his own stylish version of a top hat and cane. That vision quickly shifted to a slow handheld walker, or me rolling him down the aisle in his wheelchair... Dang!... I really wanted to find a husband fast, so at least my man would have the opportunity to meet my dad. I still think about that a lot.

All of my past boyfriends really got along with and loved my dad. He was the cool one, the entertainer. Making sure everyone had a beer or margarita in hand and if you happen to be around the house at dinnertime, of course you were invited to stay and join us, at least for an appetizer. My boyfriends would end up going out

You may not control all the events that happen to you, but you can decide not to be reduced by them. ~ Maya Angelou with just my dad for a pitcher of beer and watch the ball games at the local pubs or pizza joints. He would introduce them to the sexy, barely dressed, beer sponsor girls and always get a hug or two along with a free shot glass or bottle opener, whatever little trinket he could score. Dad had fun wherever we went. He was a good dad, and I definitely was Daddy's little girl.

He used to joke around that I was his #1 son... only because they ran out of little pink blankets in the hospital when I was born. There were so many little girls born on the same day that they introduced me to him for the first time in a blue blanket. He always encouraged me and helped me mentally and emotionally, even when it came to sex, he told me what to expect and said he didn't want me to be a prude. He ALWAYS took my side in arguments (which really pissed off my mom). She thought we were always siding against her, which unfortunately was true.

Me and Dad had a very special bond. I do think he always really wanted a son, and when my nephew Justin was born, he couldn't be happier. His eyes lit up and his smile would shine from ear to ear. I think there was a particular moment when he had Justin in his lap, laughing and smiling (we have a picture of that moment), the moment when he decided that he needed to figure out how to get himself a better quality of life.

He asked the doctors what he could do. He wanted

to have additional energy to travel with my mom and enjoy their retirement, just as they had always imagined. Dad wanted a better quality of life and spend the final years being a 'cool, fun' grandpa. So, it was mutually determined that his best option was to put in a pacemaker. Something to help his heart beat more easily so he wouldn't continually be so weak. We discussed the pros and cons of surgery and he was convinced that Justin needed a grandpa with more energy and he didn't want to be (or act) like the old man he had become.

Dad and I, lay one afternoon, quietly on his bed, just the two of us while Mom was out running errands. And as he didn't even have the energy to sit up or watch TV, he held my hand and started to talk. He asked in his very weak, insecure, unknowing voice, "Would you be able to forgive me for anything I have done to hurt you in the past?"

He never wanted to let me down, do me wrong, or be unavailable. He professed his love and hoped I thought he was a good enough father. He told me he was proud of me and I could never do any wrong in his eyes. We both shed a few tears and smiled as we continued to squeeze each other's hand.

He adored me, and we both reflected back on, laughed, and brought up some of the "secrets" we had shared over the years. Things that no one except us knew about, incidents that I promised to hold to the grave...

A meaningful life is not being rich, being popular, being highly educated or being perfect...it is about being real, being humble, being strong and being able to share ourselves and touch the lives of others.

memories that may confuse me and/or warm my heart forever. Memories to this day that I have only mentioned to a select few people. Nothing abusive, nothing strange, some people may even brag about what was done. But to us, it was just a secret. Our secret. A few little white lies, or hidden truths that weren't worth knowing or sharing with others. Nonetheless, even to this day, there are still little lies that I cannot reveal. A little secret or two that I promised to hold onto.

To Dad, we shared these secrets and it made our father/ daughter bond even stronger, although to me, in the back of my mind I knew... my dad was a liar. It was not just a secret or two, but rather a burden of responsibility. I would continue to wonder over the years what other secrets he was keeping, hiding, from me, from my mom, my sister, anyone? What else did he do that he didn't want anyone knowing about... We had a pack, a bond of secrecy, he counted on me and he knew I would never let him down.

Along with this burden of being his 'secret keeper', my responsibility of keeping this special bond to feel loved, I had another big problem with my dad. It grew over time and I really wasn't aware of it until later in life once I was an adult.

He liked to take things. He felt entitled to things. I remember him and Mom fought about his stealing escapades when I was a kid and I even heard that he got kicked out of a few department stores and wasn't allowed back inside. He would love giving gifts to people, and after I found out that he hadn't really purchased any of those nice gifts, I felt really bad taking them from him or giving them to my friends. It was hard to tell my dad I didn't want those things, I didn't need those things. As I thought back to all those times he had offered me, my friends and my family gifts and trinkets.

> *I wonder if he was trying to buy my love. I wonder if he believes he is entitled to our love like he feels entitled to all those "things". Does he not feel worthy? Why wouldn't he just work for, earn and pay for those things... he had the money... does he feel that he cannot earn our love?*

I was a bit confused about his values, and concerned it would be genetic. I knew it was wrong, but, did he have a good cause or reason? Are we all entitled? Is this what you do when you are unable to obtain what you want? I knew better... my dad just had a problem.

I thought about the time shortly after he came back from a trip to Israel with a bunch of beautiful items and jewelry; Mom shot me over that look... that look of disgust as she rolled her eyes wondering if I would pick up on it. I asked him if he had the receipts. When he couldn't produce any of them, I asked him to donate all the items to the local temple and told him that I was

Never forget the people who take time out their day to check up on you.

disappointed in him. He was embarrassed and tried to just forget it ever happened. I think back now and perhaps convinced myself that is why when we were growing up, he really loved bringing the family and going to those craft fairs where they would put out little baskets of rings, rocks, trinkets for whoever was passing by to fumble through and make an impulse purchase. It wasn't as though these little baskets of things had a lot of value, they were more of the teaser items to get you to look at the more expensive stuff. And always to my surprise, Dad would continue to come home with a pocket full of cool "stuff". I used to think of how considerate he was, getting things for me, my sister, Mom and our friends... none of the other parents would just hand out gifts like my dad. He would act like he searched long and hard and finally found this special item for one of my friends and say, why don't you give it to them for his or her birthday?

Towards the last few years of his life, just before he became wheelchair bound, Mom, Dad, and I went to another local crafts festival. We all walked around together and passed the food vendors, the air brush painters and the jewelry makers. We all paused and after some time being mesmerized by the glass blower, we looked up and somehow Mom and I were still standing there separated from Dad who had wandered off, so I went to go look for him.

I saw him across one of the aisles. As I stood to watch,

he picked up this, looked at that. I continued to watch from a distance, observing him fiddling through another one of those ring baskets... and then, right in front of me, I saw it... I watched him take a handful and slip it into his pocket. I just witnessed one of my Dad's little entitlement actions. I couldn't believe what I just saw and I, with agitation in my voice, approached him and said, "Put them back."

He looked me straight in the eye and said, "What?"

I said, "Put them back."

"What is it that you think I have?"

I said, "Whatever you just put into your pocket."

He said, "There isn't anything in my pocket."

I took a step toward him as he pulled away.

"I don't know what you think you saw, but you are mistaken. I didn't take anything," he insisted.

I stood there dumbfounded with a blank stare on my face.

How could my DAD look me straight in the eye and lie to me? What else did he lie to me about? Now, I know what I saw, I know his past, I know what he is capable of... Why would he lie... to me? I'm daddy's #1 son, his little girl, the apple of his eye... and he just

While we try to teach our children all about life, our children teach us what life is all about. ~ Angela Schwindt *lied straight to my face. WOW!*

I shook my head and was in total disbelief, and just walked away. How could he lie to ME, when I'm the one who knows some of his darkest secrets?

Episodes like that just stick with you... I'm not sure what I was supposed to learn or do about it, but it's something you don't just forget.

Help people, even when you know they can't help you back.

Chapter 04

~Death~

What a great week, I just got picked up at the airport by my good friend Carol, we talked about all that had went on while I was visiting my goddaughter in Barnhart, Missouri, we laughed and told stories. It was a long, late flight, the last of the day, so I had on my shorts, a comfy t-shirt, and my flip flops. She dropped me off at the top of the stairs from my condo, we waved good bye, said goodnight, and she drove off. I rolled my suitcase, clunking down the stairs, slowly one at a time toward the entrance to my condo.

It was actually a very chilly, raining evening, the fog had already rolled in. I loved the way the rain danced in the rays of the streetlight. As my eyes followed the raindrops whisking across the kitchen window, I noticed a light on inside my unit. This was strange, since my roommate worked the graveyard shift.

Now, Christian was the coolest roommate ever. He loved to clean, cook, and help out around the house and yard. He was very mechanical and liked to take things apart and put them back together so they worked even better. We had a long history of friendship. He had been my roommate for over five years. He was great on the BBQ preparing anything from steak, veggies, and corn to kabobs, lobsters, and burgers... Always a yummy treat. He mentioned that he wasn't very close with his family while growing up and hardly ever saw them. But, then after about two years as my roommate, he reunited with his sisters and father. He was thrilled to get together with them and recently, all of us coordinated little lunches and get togethers as often as possible.

Christian and his dad started bonding by going to the junkyard where he picked up all types of car parts. He started selling them on E-bay and making some decent money. Before I knew it, my garage was filled with FedEx boxes, labels, and car parts... I couldn't tell what was coming or going. He also started buying those toy Hot Wheels cars... big, small it didn't matter, he would buy them in bulk, repackage them and sell them for a few bucks more than he had purchased them for.

He loved my dog Kodi. Kodi was a big 90 pound Chinese Foo Dog... the dog you often see depicted in those jade statues sitting outside Chinese restaurants. They are sometimes called the celestial or Lion Dog. He was very regal and majestic. Kodi and Christian would take walks on the golf course where we lived. This is where I had purchased my first condo. Which I saved for, for basically my entire life.

My dream was to live on the beach, but that was not affordable on a single income, so I settled for a cute two bedroom condo on a golf course which I decorated to make feel like home, and it was. My foster son enjoyed living there and it was conveniently close to work. My favorite was relaxing on the sofa looking at my 285 gallon saltwater aquarium that took over a year to get established. Kodi had made lots of doggie friends and me with their parents and had a group of us who took several walks throughout the day together. Kodi would occasionally escape from the front door to take a run across the golf course and into the local swamp. Kodi enjoyed chasing the bunnies, and Christian enjoyed picking up the lost golf balls... another hobby of his. He could find 50-100 golf balls a day and sell them on E-bay. Dang!... People will buy anything for the right price.

They would both come back to the house so filthy and stinky from the swamp, I'd kick them both into the shower. Kodi loved the water, the beach, and getting a bath. For a big fluffy dog, bathing was an ordeal. To make sure he was thoroughly rinsed was a chore, and then brushing and drying the double coat... it took over three hours. One day, Christian had a great idea and the three of us went out and upstairs into the garage... we pulled out the 'shop vac' and started vacuuming him. WOW! What a difference, he shined and the house wasn't left like a Kodi Dog fur carpet. We started vacuuming him 2-3 times a week. Kodi loved

So many people are scared of being hurt that they close themselves off from being loved.

it and so did Christian. Christian thrived on positive reinforcement and compliments, he was always trying to help out any way he could. With his extra E-bay money he was really helping out with the rent.

The Real Estate market was just killing me. It was so slow and at this time, I had about 8-12 short sale files sitting on the desks over at the bank waiting for an asset manager's approval to move forward. For the first time in my life, money wasn't easily coming in and I was struggling to pay the bills.

When things were financially good for me, two and three years ago, when Christian didn't have a job, I allowed him to stay in my guest room for free while I created and spiffed-up a custom resume which quickly got him a good job hanging and fixing widow covers and blinds. It was something he had some experience doing in the past, and was pretty good at. Within about eight months, the company stopped paying him and went belly up. We adjusted his resume and got him an interview over at Costco where they hired him for the graveyard shift stocking merchandise. He loved and thrived at that job. He made friends, kept busy, was able to use his hands, and get plenty of exercise. Within a short amount of time he was promoted and eventually after a few years it recently came up in conversation that he was being recommended for a management position. He was so excited. I had helped him turn him into the perfect roommate. Slept during the day, worked at night. He would clean and watch Kodi when I was out. He didn't really even have any friends come by, he just focused on reconnecting with his family and making money.

So, back to that chilly, foggy, raining night... While I clanked my suitcase down the wet stairs I noticed the upstairs neighbor was doing their laundry and the scent of their fabric softener sheets was strong in the air. I walked through the strong scented steam and as I took a deep breath in, I opened my condo door... "PEEYOO!"

The stench was almost unbearable. The dishes were stacked up in the sink, the lights were on, the TV not blasting, but pretty loud for 11:30 p.m. "Hey Bubba!" (we used to call each other) I yelled, "what's up? It smells like something died in the sink."

Kodi ran to the front door to greet me, but something was wrong. He was damp, and not from the rain, he was panting heavily and circling me as if to get me moving down the hallway and herding me into the house. "Hey, Christian," I yelled again, "can you turn down the TV? What the heck is that smell?"

As I walked down the hallway with Kodi panting at my side, the smell at this point was making me nauseous. "I think a rat died in the attic or the kitchen. Can't you smell it?"

I noticed the ottoman was in the middle of the living room. I took a hold of Kodi's collar and he pulled me

We can not change the past, but we can start a new chapter with a happy ending.

towards the TV. I kicked off my flip flops, parked my suitcase and checked to see if Christian was asleep on the sofa. To my shock, surprise and devastation, I saw legs poking out behind the ottoman face up and I quickly hopped down the stairs to check.

It was Christian lying dead on my living room floor.

Now, I know you have seen those goofy horror movies where the crazy teenage girl is screaming like a psycho and you think that could never be me... I would be calm, dial 911, and never react that hysterically... Let me just say, NOT!

"OH MY GOD... HE'S DEAD!" I was screaming as if I was telling Kodi something he didn't already know. This was not the just lay down with your eyes closed like you just fell asleep dead, this was worse than anything I had ever seen, heard about or even imagined. My heart was pounding out of my chest. Kodi looked at me for assurance, he had stayed by Christian's side for... Oh my, I had no idea how long. I ran back into the hallway where I'd parked my suitcase, grabbed my cell phone from my purse and immediately dialed 911. As the operator answered, I was shaking in terror. "Oh MY GOD, he's dead! I don't know what to do, he's DEAD! Come over here, HE'S DEAD!" I was screaming into the phone

Challenges are what make life interesting and overcoming them is what makes life meaningful.

~ Joshua Marine

again to the 911 operator.

"Are you sure?" asked the operator.

Oh my gosh, I thought to myself, do I really need to go back and check... he looked pretty dead to me. I ran back over to his empty vessel of a body with phone in one hand and Kodi's collar in the other... the smell alone was hideous, his eyes, wide open, blood red with a large black hole of a pupil leading to what used to be his soul. Yellow foam oozed from his nose and mouth into a pool of what could have been vomit on the carpet to his side. Urine, feces, blood... his body not of any color I had ever seen.

Indescribable shades of blue, purple, green, splotchy... and those eyes, I couldn't stop looking back into his eyes... It wasn't a look of sadness or pain, it was really strange... It was like there was nothing there inside of him, every ounce of life, energy, soul was gone. Swollen blood red eyes, no whites. It seemed like I stared at that body forever when I think back, but in actuality it may have only been a few seconds...

"Yes!" I screamed... "He's DEAD!"

"Is he breathing"? the operator asked again...

"NO - HE'S DEAD!" I exclaimed with frustration and passion.

"Calm down," she said, "there is an ambulance on its

It is never too late to be what you might have been. ~ George Eliot way."

"Oh My God, Oh My God, I can't believe HE's DEAD." My heart continued to pound faster and louder, I started to feel the sweat drip down my forehead into my eyes. Kodi, still in my grasp, was also panting heavily.

"Take a walk outside. I'll stay with you until they arrive," the operator said in a calm comforting voice.

As tears started streaming down my face:

> *"Oh my God, Christian... what happened to you? Oh my God, this is horrible," I kept muttering out loud to myself, to Kodi, to the 911 operator on the other end of the phone. "He's dead. He's dead."*

With my hand still clenched around Kodi's collar, we walked outside, up the stairs in front of my garage. Standing barefoot in the drizzling rain, barely seeing through the thick fog, numb with shock, I heard the ambulance. Then I saw the fire engine lights in the distance driving into the complex. They passed the entry gate and headed down the long hill toward my condo, and then they turned the wrong way.

I was definitely freaking out as I told the operator on the phone, "He's dead and they went the wrong way. Turn them around. I'm behind them, they need to turn around."

"Breathe," she said, "just breathe. I'm here with you."

"But he's dead," I said again. "He's dead." Although in a daze, waiting for what seemed like forever, the Fire Department really did get there quickly, within just a few minutes. The group got out of the truck and walked towards me. Someone started asking me questions and told me it's ok to hang up the phone. Then they asked if there was anyone else in the home and what happened.

"I don't know, I just got back from visiting my goddaughter, my suitcase is at the end of the stairs and I walked in... and... and... and He's DEAD." I was barely able to spit out the words one more time while sobbing and confused over what was transpiring in front of my very eyes.

"We're going in."

I started to follow, and they asked me to stay outside. One fireman asked, "Do you need a jacket, shoes, it's cold out here. There will be someone here shortly to talk to you, so just stay here and wait."

Still numb and not feeling a thing I responded in a very calm, almost dreamlike tone, "No... just the dog leash which should be on the counter by the front door, please."

The scene began to get blurry, almost like the fog had taken over and I was stuck in a hypnotic dream, or I should say a bad nightmare. Nothing seemed real as I stood alone under the carport in the misty rain still holding Kodi by the collar... the world around me seemed to be moving in slow motion. Was this shock? Was I dreaming? I didn't recognize anyone around me as I continued to stand with Kodi and bright RED LIGHTS KEPT FLASHING in the thick fog.

I hung up with the 911 operator and immediately called back my friend Carol who had just dropped me off... not sure if she made it home yet... all this probably transpired in less than 10 minutes. "OH MY GOSH, PLEASE COME BACK, I don't know what to do... He's dead!"

"Who, Kodi?" she asked. "No Christian."

"What?" She swallowed hard. "I'm on my way." She turned around and came over immediately. She parked her car, came over and all we could do was stand together, hug and cry. It was unbelievable. Just last weekend, a day before my trip, we had all just gone to the fair together with another friend from the office. Everything should have been fine.

What happened? The evening process took several hours and it was determined by the coroner that Christian had been lying dead in my condo for over three days.

I couldn't stay in the house that night, not until some things were taken care of. The coroner let me know that I needed to call my insurance company and have

HAZMAT come to clear the blood stained carpet and then give me the clearance to move back in. Another fireman or officer then came outside and started asking about his family and how they could reach them. Then he politely asked, "Do you have someplace to stay tonight?"

There was a short pause. "Yes," I replied. "I'll call my folks."

Hating to bother my folks so late, I think by now it was almost 2 a.m... I made the call, knowing they would freak out, too, before I even said word.

"Hello?" my mom asked in a groggy, you just woke me up, muffled voice.

"Hi, Mom." The tears came rolling again and I started to sob.

"What's wrong? What happened," she immediately asked.

I can hardly get a word out, as by this time I was totally exhausted. "You'll never guess what happened."

Her first response was, "OH NO, is it Kodi?"

I replied, "No. Christian.'"

"What about Christian?" she asked.

"He's dead."

"What?" she exclaimed in disbelief. I could hear my dad in the background asking if Kodi was dead.

"No. Tell Dad Kodi is fine... a little traumatized since he was with Christian when it happened and hasn't been outside for three days, but he will be ok. Christian on the other hand is not ok. The coroner is here with the ambulance and firemen, they want to be sure I have a place to sleep tonight. I need to call HAZMAT and the homeowner's insurance and deal with all this and his family tomorrow."

"I don't understand?" she interrupted, still sounding half asleep, and wanting to get into a conversation to get all the details right now. This was happening while I was still standing in the rain, lights flashing, with the coroner and some social services lady waiting to confirm that I have a place to sleep for the night. "Can we talk about it when I get there, or in the morning? There's a lot going on right now."

"Of course," she replied, and then started to have a conversation with my dad in the background. I realized I was still holding the phone but not saying a word. The fireman took the phone from my hand, hung it up, and set it down.

The rest of the evening seemed like a blur... like a movie that just fades into white. I was standing there one minute, and the next thing I knew, it was already a few days later.

The days passed and quickly turned into a week trying to coordinate with Christian's family, make memorial arrangements, call Costco, figure out his passwords to log onto his Facebook account, Ebay, and his other email accounts. I wanted to reply and send out some of his Ebay purchases, and inform his friends and family as to what was going on. This was an enormous undertaking. Who would have ever thought? We weren't married, we weren't even dating. I had NO access to his personal contacts or even his password on his phone. No ATM pin code, or an address in case of emergency... Lesson learned the hard way.

I needed to make the appointment with HAZMAT, my insurance company, get some new carpeting, and go back to the condo every day to feed my fish. My pride and joy. In my condo, as I mentioned, I had a 285 gallon salt water aquarium. I remember back when I first purchased the smaller 50 gallon hexagon tank with a baby eel, and he grew and grew. A few years later for the holidays, I bought myself and my growing eel a special present, a brand new tank, and it filled my entire wall. It was amazing, my tropical oasis. Sand, rocks, plants, a perfect ecosystem that I would gaze into and become mesmerized for hours. Over the years I had acquired some very beautifully colored, exotic and tropical fish. I just loved to sit at night with my meditation music playing. The blue night light on the tank would create such an amazing tranquil effect, and I'd watch

Many people never get what they want because they are too busy holding onto things they are suppose to let go.

the nocturnal snowflake eel swimming around as if he was dancing around to the music. Such a beautiful sight, up and down, around and around through the corals he would go twirling and dancing in his tranquil environment. My puffer fish would always come to the glass every morning to say hello and wiggle his pudgy cute face back and forth as if to tell me something funny had happened the night before. Watching the water and the fish was very relaxing to me, it reminded me of when I would go scuba diving in Cabo and watch all the amazing fish and colors and hear nothing... nothing except the sound of my heartbeat and my own breath. Sigh... I would love to go there right now and escape my currently chaotic world.

That week of staying on the couch at my folks' house turned quickly into a habit and before I even realized it, a few weeks had passed. I was just not comfortable staying alone in a condo that had a dead body lying there for what the coroner stated was over three days. Apparently, he'd had a brain aneurysm.

As a couple of months passed, and the devastation, shock, and disbelief started to wear off. I was getting comfortable spending the extra time with my dad. He had been sick for a long time, in and out of the hospital, and Mom really needed a break. We were lucky she could take some time off from schlepping him around to doctors' appointments and I could be there to step in.

I'm strong because I've been weak. I'm brave because I've been afraid. I'm wise because I've been foolish.

For the first time, while Dad was resting, Mom and I really started to talk to one another like adults. We would all go out together, stop for lunch, hang out together, talk about silly stuff we did in the past while growing up, old boyfriends, girlfriends, good times, and crazy conversations. We would laugh together until our bellies hurt... or Dad would start wheezing and then coughing from lack of oxygen.

When it was just me and Dad, we smiled together as he would turn up the music in my car (usually a little reggae by Bob Marley), he would ask me to put the convertible top down on the Porsche, and told me he felt like a VIP being chauffeured around town.

We tried to motivate one another by talking about sharing future good times together. Dad mentioned that he still looked forward to walking (or should I say strutting) me down the aisle... if I was to EVER find the right man. He was still convinced he would be wearing a crazy stylish top hat and cane.

And I would joke, "You mean, me pushing you down the aisle in your wheelchair and oxygen tank."

He would take a big breath in... choke a little on the way out... and just nod his head knowing everything will work itself out and it will all be okay.

learn how to have fun without alcohol. Talk without a cellphone. Love without conditions. Dream without drugs. Smile without selfies.

Our job is 'to share' knowledge with those
who have less of it, and 'to learn' what we can from
those who have a little more.
We are here 'to give' as much as we can.

~ Karen Berg

Chapter 05

~Shattered Dreams~

The day came when I finally had to walk back into my condo. I continued to sleep on the couch at Mom and Dad's, but it was the day that HAZMAT was scheduled to pull out the compromising carpeting, and the insurance company planned to replace the entire area that HAZMAT needed to remove. At the same time, Christian's family members planned to come over and rummage through all Christian's things; they chose who would get what, which things they wanted to keep of his and what would ultimately go into the dumpster. I showed them the garage, and let them know it's all for them to take, whatever they decided to leave, I would most likely throw away. It took them weeks to go through it all and decipher who got what of all his belongings. This was no easy task. From packaged car parts labeled in shipping boxes and tons of unlabeled boxes to hundreds of boxes of Hot Wheels cars, tools, packaging materials... like me, his family just didn't know what to do with it all.

As time went on, we finally attended a very nice memorial service for Christian. Costco provided the food, and his family was able to afford cremation through the Neptune Society. A fair amount of neighbors, my friends and family, and several colleagues were all in attendance. A few spectators including myself and his sister were amused with the little lizard near the podium doing push-ups as the different speakers talked about Christian's life. I still wasn't comfortable going back and sleeping at the condo by myself, I had definitely gotten into a routine at Mom and Dad's and had made myself useful taking Dad to appointments and activities to give Mom a little break.

Unfortunately, I had been a little distracted with what had been going on and let my mortgage payment slip for the past three months. With the New Year ahead I called the bank to get everything straightened out. I explained my situation to the representative, asked for forbearance (for those of you who don't know what that is, in cases of medical emergencies, tragedies, and death, the bank can take the missed payments and throw them on the back end of your mortgage loan without any penalty.)

I was told that I would not qualify, so instead I was given several payment options to choose from that would immediately reinstate my loan and keep me out of trouble.

I chose to borrow money from my mom and sister to pay a large chunk (almost all) of the money owed and little extra (a few hundred dollars) for only three months. Then, I would NOT be in, or get into a default situation. I received a few letters in the mail about refinancing, but, because I already had a great rate and over $300K in equity, I declined. I coordinated getting my payments together and sent the bank a certified check to cover the agreed upon significant portion of the amount owed. I was again assured by each representative I spoke with that my home was not in ANY jeopardy. I followed up for the next few days, even after I received the confirmation of receipt that all was good and my payments were on track. I was assured by several more representatives that I had nothing to worry about.

I received a call from the bank about a week later stating that I needed to request a refinance with my forbearance, although it wouldn't be approved because:

A) I was no longer in default, and

B) I didn't have enough current income to qualify.

The representative insisted I write a letter explaining my circumstances and specifically state in the letter that, "I have over $75K of equity." Not over $100K, not over $200, and definitely NOT OVER $300K, SPECIFICALLY THAT I HAVE OVER $75K IN EQUITY IN MY PROPERTY. Apparently, that was their magic number. Of course, as expected, a week later I received the letter stating that I was denied for the refinance/forbearance and should continue to make my monthly payment along with the extra amount for the next few months,

Just so we're all clear, it's okay to miss people you no longer want in your life. Missing someone is your heart's way of reminding you that you love them.

just like we had previously agreed upon over the phone.

Over the holidays and New Year I spent a lot of time with my folks, and in January I slowly moved my way back into my condo. Dad's condition was getting worse, business was very slow and the short sale deals that I had been waiting to get into escrow, continued to sit at the bank for indefinite amounts of time. As a Real Estate agent, with the market as crazy as it was, I spoke with various representatives on behalf of myself and my clients regularly. In fact, I spent between 4-6 hours on hold just about every day. I took diligent notes and documented all the names, transfers, completed and disconnected calls in a very orderly fashion. It was my job. Everything was starting to get back to normal, deals were closing, I was home relaxing with my fish tank, even Kodi was back to his daily routine.

All was good with the exception of Dad's health. Up and down, he was finally scheduled and then rescheduled for his pacemaker surgery. It needed to be postponed due to a previous minor cold or infection. So, at this point, we scheduled my sister and her family to be here for support and to encourage him by giving him the opportunity to interact with his grandchild prior to recovery.

About three weeks and counting... this was going to be a BIG deal. If it worked, Dad could potentially feel great and have his energy back. The cancer was in remission and his attitude was strengthening. We all thought this

Pay attention to how people act when you're not on good terms. True colors will always reveal themselves.

How to Let it Go!   Chapter 5   **86** would be a very positive thing.

I was all settled back into my now quiet condo and started to consider my possibilities and options... what to do... get another foster kid? Nah. I wanted to wait for a husband or boyfriend to help. Get another roommate? Nah, not yet, there wouldn't be anyone as cool as Christian. I decided to just focus on work and making some money. I started to dabble a little in the online affiliate marketing field, I knew it would be big in the future, everything was moving online. I purchased some video animation software and started putting together some real estate marketing videos... I thought perhaps if one of my friends could help me to edit them, we could start creating them for new agents, maybe make a little extra cash... or even become an affiliate and sell this software to other agents if they wanted to create their own videos. Ha ha ha, Pipe dream... that was way too technical and time consuming for me... that project came to a quick halt.

Sitting at the computer going through emails, checking Facebook, pretty much wasting time, I felt Kodi nudging me for his morning walk. He was ready to visit his doggie friends and play on the golf course. As I mentioned, there was a big group of us homeowners who would get together 2-3 times a day for the daily doggie pow wow and yappy hour. A little sniffing, peeing, playing, chasing, and walking around our complex. What a good life, to be my dog! I opened my

I believe in the ocean curing all bad moods, I believe in the waves wiping away worries, I believe in seashells bringing good luck, I believe in toes in the sand grounding my soul.

door on the morning of March 16th and there was a note posted on my screen door.

"Your house has been sold at auction. You have 3 days to move out!"

WHAT? They have got to be kidding.

I called the bank with all my account information and the rep said that she had no idea what to do. I asked for a supervisor, and her response was, "Oops! I think your file ended up on the wrong desk."

"OOPS? That is not acceptable. What do I do?"

"Nothing," she said. "It's too late, your home has already been sold."

"Excuse me, but, I am fully aware of rescinding an auction and giving a house back to the homeowner. Especially if it was because of an OOPS."

"Sorry," she said, "at this point there is nothing I can do."

Holy crap! Who should I call? My first response was to call my broker and ask if she had a recommendation for a good attorney, then call my title reps, other agents, and then my mom. "Hey, Mom, you are never gonna believe this, but the bank sold my house at auction yesterday and they want me out in three days."

"Can they do that?" she asked.

"I don't know, but they are doing it."

Just a few months after I borrowed all the money to pay the defaulted amount.

We had a deal. I have it in writing, they can't just take my house away... I'm not upside down, it should never have gone to auction. I have over $300K of equity. All I could think of is why me? I've got to take on this NOW! I wonder how much they sold it for... Why the HELL did they sell it?

I looked online and the bank sold my home for 1¢ over what I owed on the property. Can you believe it? What a deal this investor got... an immediate $300K+ of equity. No additional money needed, it wasn't even a flip. It was move in ready... it was my HOME. Not cool. Not cool at all. I spent the afternoon on the phone talking to several attorneys and interviewed over six who were anxious to take on my case...

They all said, "It's a no brainer, you will win, and probably get one of the bank's other bank foreclosures, too." One attorney asked me and my mother out loud, "Did you want one or two beachfront properties?" They chuckled as what was just explained to them was a ridiculous action on the part of the bank. I had all my documents in order, who I spoke with, the faxed deal that was made, the deposited bank checks, the certified payment receipt, all the letters.

A strong woman will automatically stop trying if she feels unwanted. She won't fix it or beg, she'll just walk away.

I wanted the best of the best, whichever firm was most recommended. Whomever had taken on my bank in the past, and won the case. And, who was able and competent to help me get my home back! Mom and I went down to the attorney's office, spoke with their representative and signed the paperwork, $30K retainer seemed like a lot of money, but losing my home and over $300k of equity... we both agreed that we had to do it.

The attorneys advised me that the more hassles I went through, the more money I spent fixing this issue, the more money they would be able to get me in the lawsuit. He suggested I pick the most expensive hotel/resort and put it on my credit card and stay for two months...

"That's ok", I cut him off mid sentence, "I'll just stay with my folks."

Now that I was back settled into my condo, I didn't really want to leave again. I was getting tired of living out of a suitcase on Mom and Dad's couch, and I finally stopped feeling like a tourist in my own home. They told me that I could take my time, there was no rush, they needed to file a Lis Pendense in order to officially kick me out. The attorneys told me to just stay put and once they contacted my bank, everything would be back to normal in about two months. I didn't need to start planning my move, and within two months top I was promised, "You will be back in your own home. Don't worry."

Soon enough, the Lis Pendense arrived at my door. I

Don't waste your time trying to get people to love you. Spend your time with those who already do.

immediately scanned it and sent it over to my attorneys to handle. Confirmed it was received and asked what I do next... they said, "Wait."

Well I waited, and waited, called speaking with the attorney at least once every day. I was getting nervous, I have never been good at waiting... I am a doer, an action taker. I was never very good at sitting around. I didn't even sit around when talking on the phone. I would pace. Back and forth, around in circles, through the kitchen, up and down the hall... always moving. My mom used to joke around and tell me to, "Stand still!" I think she thought I was hyper active or now what they probably would have diagnosed me with what would be ADD or ADHD. My mind was constantly churning and various scenarios would race through my head. Should I be here when it happens, should I be out, what about my stuff? Will they let me coordinate getting it back, could they just rummage through it all... I felt trapped in my own house. I never knew anyone who actually got kicked out of their house. Even with my short sale clients, I worked them deals to get paid to move, plenty of time to coordinate, or we just sold their home and they moved out after escrow. After further discussion with my attorneys they kept insisting that the more money and expenses that I was able to incur, the more money they would be able to help me recover.

Now, I'm all good with getting money, but at this point, with all my current business short sale files still sitting on

Being with no one is better than being with the wrong one. Sometimes, those who fly solo have the strongest wings.

another desk down the hall, I didn't have much to just go frivolously spend. I was being very particular on where it went, and I didn't want any EXTRA expenses that may or may not be returned in the lawsuit. I thought I was already spending way too much on the monthly retainer for these attorneys, but didn't feel I had any other choice. These guys were supposedly the best and had promised to get me back into my home.

In the next few days, I received a voice mail from my attorney saying that we were in trouble and I needed to pay some guy additional money to postpone my eviction. He said, "Trust me, it's really important!"

So, I immediately called the guy who could prevent the eviction and he let me know that at any moment the sheriff could come by and kick me out, or the locksmith could come by and change the locks. I asked, "What happens to Kodi?"

He said that they would probably bring him to the shelter. "Absolutely not!" I was never going to let that happen. Kodi would be happier staying at my parents' house with their dog.

The stress of getting kicked out and causing a scene in my community was overwhelming, more than I'd like to admit. So, I bit the bullet, took the advice of my attorneys and paid for the guy to postpone the eviction and at the same time prepared to move out of my home.

How beautiful it is to stay silent when someone expects you to be enraged.

I hired the movers, found a storage unit... my big dilemma was what to do with my 285 gallon salt water fish tank. Wow! Those are some of my most vivid memories. I couldn't help just imagining myself...

Watching the handheld nets circle around my tank capturing my little fishes. I can see the eyes of my cute puffer fish look at me as if he was saying, "Don't let them take me." I could imagine hearing my still growing, happy eel ask, "What did I do to make you not want me anymore?" Tears started welling up into my eyes. I felt like my world was again coming to an end. What was I going to do with my tank?

I couldn't just pick them up and throw them in the car. Argh! Another problem to tackle. The attorney advised I coordinate with a pet store to pay them rent for a few months to hold it for me, again reminding me that the more I spend, the more I could ask for in damages. Fortunately, after calling around, the guy who originally helped me set it up had his own shop and said he would watch my babies until my housing situation worked itself out. What a life saver (Thank you, Len)!

Now let me tell you, this set up with the fish, corals, sea rocks and the tank cost me around $10,000. This was no little fish tank. It took four guys, a huge truck and more than five hours to disassemble, drain, catch my babies and pack them up for the move. It was an entire

I see and appreciate all the beauty that surrounds me. I am grateful for all things big and small that make my world beautiful. I don't take for granted the humble, the simple, or the quiet.

process that took months to set up correctly and lots of education to maintain. That was one of my greatest fears and what really upset me the most out of this totally unexpected, horrible situation. It was not being able to see my fishes and enjoy and relax with my swimming fishy family on a daily basis. I did plan to stop by the shop every week to visit them and make sure they were doing ok. The first week, I managed to stop by the shop three times after Dad's doctor appointments while he was napping.

Okay, I felt a tiny bit of relief. The attorneys were supposedly taking care of the bank to get my house back, my parents were taking care of Kodi, my fish guy was now taking care of my other babies, and everything I owned had been moved into a 10x20 storage unit from floor to ceiling without access to anything at all. Nothing labeled. Nothing marked. All I had were the broken promises from my very well paid attorneys, still convincing me, that I would be able to put it all back in approximately a month.

Living out of a small overnight bag, sleeping on my parents' couch was not quite my idea of the best or most comfortable night's sleep, but at least we were all together and the anxiety of the unknown was not hovering at the forefront of my mind.

At this point it was really only a matter of hours until the locks on my unit were changed and days until the new investor started making changes to my unit. I went by and took photos of how it was, so just in case the investor did make any changes, I could put it back to the way it used to be. I wanted to be sure I would be able to get it back to MY HOME. After Christian's death, just three months earlier, I had just repainted, redecorated. It was again, a perfect place for me to call HOME.

My sister and her family came into town for Dad's surgery. Unfortunately, they wouldn't let kids into the hospital, so my sister brought photos of Dad's special grandkid into the hospital room. Dad was awake, made jokes about people as he liked to do, was very interactive, alert and looking forward to his new opportunity of living with a pacemaker, having the energy to do the things he wanted to do, and going to the places he wanted to see.

You see, Mom and Dad's last planned vacation didn't turn out anything like they had planned or hoped it would. They flew across the world to go on their first Mediterranean cruise. Before they knew what had happened, my dad was checked into the local hospital in Venice, Italy. They were of course both very disappointed that the only part of Europe they actually were able to see was the airport and the inside of the hospital along with the hospital cafeteria. While sitting with the family by his side, Dad spoke again of going back to the Mediterranean after he regained his strength as this was something they were both very excited about doing.

Sometimes the memory of someone is better than the reality of them. ~ Steve Maraboli

The energy in THIS hospital room was different, overall there was an upbeat sense of confidence and determination. A different excited energy surrounded my Dad. It wasn't the same agitated, frustrated Dad who deeply wanted to be on a cruise in the Mediterranean and instead was stuck trying to get back home to his regular doctor. Here, Dad seemed at ease, the family positive and all together, kisses, hugs, winks, and smiles... then they rolled him into the operating room.

Several hours later we get the call that the surgery was a success. Back at the hospital we visited Dad who, much to our surprise, was now having these severe twitches which the doctor called minor seizures. He said they were due to one of the medications they put him on. It frustrated my dad that all of a sudden he could not eat by himself, finish speaking in full sentences and had these severe random shakes and twitches. A few days went by and they didn't get any better; in fact, it seemed like they started to get worse, he would talk and then drift off someplace else, he would start to do or say something, have a twitch attack and then lay his head down in disgust with himself.

We spoke with the doctor who decided to take him off the medication that was causing the seizures. We thought it best that he become sedated during the healing process so he wouldn't get so agitated and pull out the breathing tubes or IV. As Dad's twitches began to subside, he still would fade in and out of consciousness

Spend your time on those that love you unconditionally. Don't waste it on those that only love you when the conditions are right for them.

as the sedation medication took effect. Before the three of us packed up and went home for the evening, we gave him hugs, kisses and the three of us stood over him and prayed. We would meditate together and gave him all kinds of healing blessings and positive energies that in the past we all knew and believe had worked so well.

Early the next morning, we got the call from the hospital that things had taken a turn, and we rushed to the hospital. We stood around my dad, all hooked up to the machines that were keeping him alive. My mom and sister went to sit by the window while we waited for the doctor. I stood by the bedside holding my dad's hand watching the numbers on the monitor. It was just as quiet as the day we lay together in his room, talking about forgiveness, secrets, and the bonds between us. This was the time, the moment when time stood still... it was too quiet, it was sad... what was happening to my dad, was he ready to leave us?

His biggest fear was the ocean. He had nightmares of drowning and mentioned how he thought the sea was very ominous. The doctor came in and told us how his lungs had filled with fluids and he would eventually...

I started tuning it all out, it was too horrible to hear, "drown in his own breath." All we could do was keep him from being in pain. At this point his breaths became more and more shallow, his oxygen levels were slowly

Never blame anyone in your life. Good people give you happiness. Bad people give you experience. Worst people give you a lesson. Best people give you memories.

dropping. My eyes were filling up with tears, I could feel the knot in my stomach getting bigger and bigger. My breaths became more shallow and the tears started to drip faster and faster down my cheeks. I looked up, across the room and softly muttered out to my mom and sister... "It's time."

I motioned to Mom and my sister to come over to me, so we could all be standing all together for his moment of passing. We all told him we loved him and it was okay to go. The doctor stood by our side and let us know that the only thing keeping him alive was the pacemaker. Then quietly asked, "Is it time to turn off the machines?"

With tears pouring down all of our faces, we knew his quality of life was not and would never be what he would have wanted it to be, his brain was dying, he couldn't breathe, his abilities would never return.

Let us go, Dad. Let yourself go... No more pain, no more suffering, go to heaven, go to God, and know we love you and you will be missed tremendously. You can look down on us and shine your light on us to let us know you are okay.

The three of us muttered a little Misheberach (a Jewish prayer) under our tears, squeezed each other's hands and stood still for several minutes. Such a somber moment as the doctor unplugged all the machines, we just all stood motionless with puffy faces and tears flowing, looking for comfort in each other's eyes, and all we could see was sadness, hurt, and loss.

My sister and I needed to be strong for Mom. She had never lived on her own... guess it was a good thing I was now living on her couch, again. I could be there for support, encouragement, help with the logistical details and notification of our friends and family. I took in a big breath and let out a long sign... Uhhhgg, where to start?

Dear God, I wanna take a minute not to ask for anything from you. But simply to say Thank Your for all I have.

Life is

an opportunity, benefit from it.

Life is a beauty, admire it.

Life is a dream, realize it.

Life is a challenge, meet it.

Life is a duty, complete it.

Life is a game, play it.

Life is a promise, fulfill it.

Life is sorrow, overcome it.

Life is a song, sing it.

Life is a struggle, accept it.

Life is a tragedy, confront it.

Life is an adventure, dare it.

Life is luck, make it.

Life is life, fight for it!

~ Mother Terresa

~Promises & Disappointments~

T hank God my sister and her family were around to help. We made a long list of everything that needed to be done, and people who needed to be called and notified. I think we handled it all very well despite the sadness and disappointment that filled the house. As the next few days passed, we continued to take care of calls and arrangements, when we suddenly got interrupted by a call from my aunt. Now, my mom and her sister talk, not as frequently as they would like and usually when they do there is always something important to discuss. Mom got on the phone and all we heard was, "Oh Shit, Oh Shit!" My sister shot a dirty look across the room to Mom as my little nephew was playing nearby. It was about my grandmother, she wasn't doing so well either.

So the day arrives, we get ready for Dad's funeral. A very somber, tranquil day. We sit quietly in the car with tissues, wiping each tear that drips down our cheeks. After parking, we are greeted by family members who hug and offer their condolences. Relatives we see at weddings and funerals and seldomly in between. The smell of fresh cut grass fills the air and we are shortly escorted across the lawn into our canopy covered seats.

My friends from grade school through college are there for support. Each recollecting a positive memory, as my dad was "the cool dad" providing drinks, gifts, hugs, and laughs to all he encountered. Funerals to me are a place to remember, remember the good, put the bad in a box, and never mention the ugly... as it is now never able to repeat itself again. It was a day of reflection and solitude. Even though I was surrounded by friends and family, I felt a little alone. My phone kept giving me several chimes of notifications, as I knew there was another place where I was also needed and requested to be.

This day, unfortunately, was the exact same day and time as a longtime friend, ex business partner, ex boyfriend's court trial. This was where I was requested by him and his mom to testify on his behalf. You may wonder what was I needed to testify about... Whooa, someone else's life that was filled with drama and deceit.

Here I speak of a man whom at one time I deeply loved. Over 15 years of an on and off friendship, exclusive relationship, business partnership, lovers, and enemies. This is someone who I thought would be in my life forever. I loved his family, and truly believed they all loved mine. It wasn't until the day the police came knocking on my door and I found out that all the items moved from his old apartment into mine and my storage unit were all stolen. It wasn't until I drove over to the hotel room in our car where I found him cheating on me with another woman. The day when he jumped up, grabbed the keys out of my hand, and took the car leaving me standing in that hotel room with the other woman. It wasn't until I watched him walk out the door with my expensive High Definition Professional Canon Movie Camera, hand held professional work camera and other items that filled his oversized, overstuffed duffel bag. As he walked to his car denying he had taken or done anything wrong.

This, my friend, my lover, the man whom I had hoped was my life partner and soul mate, was a lying, cheating, stealing... S%O#B! You get the idea.

I bet you're thinking, it looks and sounds like I ended up falling for someone exactly like my dad. Big Sigh... Yup.

Now, imagine this... we had history, history of love and caring, years of friendship and support... how it turned into him and his mother calling, texting, pleading and requesting that I testify on HIS behalf on the day of my father's funeral is beyond my worst nightmare...

Maybe she doesn't know what day it is. Maybe all she is thinking of is her son. Maybe she knows I would say anything or thinks I would lie for him in court. She knows I care. Will she hate me if I don't respond? I can't respond. I can't leave. I cant be in two places at the same time, I'm at my Dad's funeral. What more could I do?

To-Do list for today: 1) Count my blessings 2) Practice kindness 3) Let go of what I can't control 4) listen to my heart 5) Be productive yet calm 6) just breathe

I tried to put all that out of my mind. I didn't want to think of my empty condo, the attorneys fighting to get my home back, the memory of the last funeral I had just attended of my dear roommate Christian. Then, of course, I started to think of my cousin Chrissy.

Are they all together? Are they in heaven celebrating... or are they just rotting in the ground, and is my dad soon to become bug food? I wish they could send me a sign. I need a sign. I need to know things are going to be okay. I need to know what to do... "God?" I questioned, "what more do you want from me?"

My mind wandered again as the group of friends and family were settling in to their seats. As I glanced over to my high school friends, I couldn't help but remember those cheerleading tryouts. The one Chrissy so diligently helped me prep for. My mind was wandering again... I thought back to those practices and rehearsals just before the tryouts. I was "So" ready. It was something I wanted "So" badly and worked "SO" hard to achieve. I remember how I stayed late, after rehearsals were done, just to help a few of the other girls get a better grasp on the routine. I helped some with their jumps and gave them tips on how to improve their height and arm positions. The instructor and lead cheerleader watched and smiled as she saw how well I worked with the other potential team members. I asked her to review my routine and give me ANY feedback SHE thought would help. She just commented, "You have nothing to worry about. You've got it, girl!" All I wanted at that time, back then, was to be a high school cheerleader. At that moment I was just led over to my seat, handed a rose to put on Dad's grave, and started to feel even more sad, alone and defeated.

The service began and the Rabbi (one of my mom's cousins) started the eulogy and kept talking about my dad and what a great man he was... WAS?... I was hurt. My dad IS a great man, just because he's gone, didn't make him not a great man any more, well I guess it did. The rest of the service was a blur. My mind couldn't concentrate on anything that was happening. The details, the family, my friends, the reception. I think we had food and I remember creating a big video memorial that was enjoyed by many. As the day passed in a fog, the guests started to disperse and head home. Eventually, the reception room cleared out and some people followed us to the house. I didn't want to believe he was really gone.

My dad. My rock. My support. I knew my sister was soon to go back home to her family and I would be left with Mom... how will we manage? We are both adults... now with Dad gone, will she still treat me like I'm 12? Ughhh. The thought just made me sick.

Breathe... Breathe... I keep telling myself. Take a deep breath and wipe the tears. Feeling overwhelmed

I forgive people. It doesn't mean I accept their behavior or trust them. It means I forgive them for me, so I can let go and move on with my life.

with what's been going on is expected, how am I going to handle all that is going on around me in my world? I need help, I need support, I need a little encouragement... Oh my gosh... I just need to sit.

A few friends stuck around and we began to talk about the good old days of valley parties, Dad helping us TP (toilet paper) friends' houses, and his famous margarita parties. Married friends ask about my 'dude' and I tried to just ignore those comments so I wouldn't get embarrassed that I was "still" single, or bring up unnecessary drama about my terrible choices. Relatives would ask, why aren't you married. Guess I just choose the wrong men, would be my quick response. A few long time, closer friends continued their support and started changing subjects. "Remember when? Did you hear what happened to so and so? I ran into someone from high school and you would never believe..."

As I listened to my friends try to take my mind off of my current situation, it must have worked because my mind started to wander back into the thoughts in my head.

I couldn't help but think of one of the times Dad, Mom, and I were driving in the car to dinner one night, laughing and chit chatting about growing old, signs from God, signs from beyond the grave after someone has passed. We talked about what we could do if something happened to one of us that would ensure we knew the other was okay in the next life. As crazy as my family is, we tried to think of something that doesn't regularly happen, like hitting a green light on the way to the funeral, to winning a lottery ticket... and we came up with a pretty disgusting sign... we talked about a big bird flying overhead and pooping on us... I laughed and said, "Yup! I can just imaging me walking down the aisle at my wedding with a big crow flying overhead." I had always wanted a destination wedding. Then, we all joked that all of a sudden a huge poop would come falling from the sky and end up dripping down the side of my white lace dress. That would be Dad, joining me at my wedding. Dad commented, "Imagine, me walking with you down the aisle as Bird Poop." We laughed, and tried to think of other signs that would work, but, be a little less gross.

Just then, my pleasant thoughts of poop and Dad were interrupted by the hug and kiss of an old high school friend, with what I'm sure he thought was a funny comment to take my mind off my dad... remember "so and so" that cheerleader from high school? She got so fat, she's now divorced, and I ran into her at the market... He just chuckled and laughed trying to make me smile.

Maybe home is nothing but two arms holding you tight when you're at your worst. ~ Yara Bashraheel

We all get heavier as we get older because
there's a lot more information in our heads.
So, tell yourself that you're not fat,
you're just really intelligent and your head
couldn't hold any more so
it started filling up the rest of you.

~ Unknown

Chapter 07

~Falling Over The Edge~

Now, I know I've brought up these Cheerleading tryouts several times, obviously they were a big deal in my little life. I loved performing. I loved creating new routines. I loved dancing! I shared this dream with Chrissy, my friends, my family... they would all cheer me on and in my mind and theirs, they not only gave me their support and encouragement, they thought I would be an awesome captain and bring our team to winning competitions.

Well... I keep bringing it up, because for some random reason, that I still to this day don't know... I didn't make the team. Whether I wasn't tall enough, blonde enough, pretty enough... I just don't know. This is where my belief of "Not Being/Doing/Having Enough" comes into my world and becomes part of my reality. A blonde girl who messed up really bad in tryouts, made the team. Another girl who froze up doing the fight song routine made the team. All the girls in Mr. Hall's math class made the team. I nailed the routine. I smiled, pointed toes, kicked high, displayed perfect jumps... and after spending weeks after class teaching the routine to some of the "less competent" girls to show my teamwork and support... they all made the team. And I didn't. Was I sad? Yes! Was I angry? Hell YES! Was I in total disappointment and in shock? Absolutely. I have been trying to "get over it" for over 30 years. Where the hell is the manual for "getting over it, and letting it go?" That's what they should have taught us in high school.

As a teenager, I thought my life in high school or as I knew it was ruined... and, it pretty much was. I was dissed by the popular group. My friends since grade and junior high school were no longer talking to me. I was no longer invited to go hang out with my jock and cheerleader friends. They didn't have time for me, they didn't want to study together after school, or go to parties together on the weekends. They had created their own exclusive group, and I was no longer a part of it. I felt very isolated and left out. This was when my self-esteem dropped significantly.

I didn't feel like I was ENOUGH. Not good enough, not pretty enough, not popular enough, not tall enough, not blonde enough... I not only started to doubt my abilities, my friends, but I generally started to have doubt in myself. I really ended up hating high school and did whatever I could to avoid interacting with many of my old friends who no longer had time for me. I remember feeling physically sick to my stomach every morning when we would drive to school, once we pulled off the freeway off ramp, took the right turn, before we would

My goal is to build a life I don't need a vacation from.

even get around the corner. Ughh, my stomach tightened up, I had a headache and I felt like I was going to puke.

I focused my mind on my work at the temple and hung out with my one best friend who I still love to this day. I started interacting with new people that were in different grades. Met a few surfers and started ditching class with them at recess to head over to Zuma Beach. I learned to surf and my passion for dancing and performing quickly switched to water sports and the ocean...

Guess what? I have carried that anger, sadness, frustration and disappointment around for what could have been almost forever. It has affected me in everyday life. It has affected my decisions, my choices, my confidence. A friend from high school would say several times over the years, "Get over it", or "Just Let it Go." As much as I wanted to, I just didn't know how. It plagued me. It had defined me. I was the loser from high school who had such potential and basically failed... and I had no idea how to let that feeling go.

I was told, "Give it to GOD."

"OK, here, GOD. It's for you. Take my pain, show me the lessons, it's all for some good reason. I don't need to know what that reason is. I just don't want to be sad, miserable, angry, hurt, or feel betrayed anymore."

That didn't seem to work. I just felt stuck and wanted to go and crawl back into bed, close my eyes and imagine

Infatuation is when you find someone who is absolutely perfect. Love is when you realize they aren't perfect and it doesn't matter.

another magical perfect place of bliss. A place where I am at peace, and happy. A place where I can share and receive love. I just closed my eyes and took another deep breath.

I started to doze off and imagined Cabo, walking on the sandy beach with an iced coffee in hand, toes just getting a bit wet as the tide crept up... a few steps toward the rocks and I could see my little puffer fish, shaking his head as to say he missed me and reminded me of some fun that had happened the night before. I felt at peace, I felt warm. The stress of the day had left and I was free picking up little sea shells, smelling the salt air, and feeling the warm rays of the sun kiss my freckled skin... Then a hand on my shoulder jolted me out of my peaceful vision.

As it was time for goodbyes and almost everyone was ready to head back home from Dad's funeral, a heavy feeling of uncertainty filled the air. Now what's next? My sister and her family would be soon be heading back home to their lives, I would be continuing my work with the attorneys to get my home back, there would be no more daily doctor visits, no more cleaning up after Dad who managed to drop something that shattered across the kitchen floor.

Now what? Such a large gap, a stressfully lacking life now filled with even more nothingness. We all arrived home, sat down on the back patio and it was very quiet. No one talked, no one really cried... We all just sat thinking about things in our minds and remembered, reminisced, and just sighed.

The silence was broken up by my sister letting me and Mom know it was time for her to pack up the car and head home. She stood up and walked inside while Mom and I stayed outside on the patio getting fresh air and taking in the view. We continued to talk about what was going to happen next. Mom was going to focus on her painting, and wanted to be alone, I was going to go out for a drive, just to escape and watch some waves.

I checked again to make sure Mom was going to be ok. She said she just wanted to be alone... to cry and to scream. She had never been alone before. She had moved in with my father directly from living with her parents, got married, had kids... She didn't know what it was going to be like. She didn't know what to expect. She was scared, lonely, excited, nervous... all those things... I was concerned, and I also knew once she had some time, I would be back to help her out. We stood up and I put my hand on Mom's shoulder to show my support, and give her a big hug. Then, to my surprise, I saw what looked like a long little green/gray worm or booger on her jacket...

"What's that...? Oh My God! It's a baby hummingbird poop."

Mom shook her head in disbelief. "I don't remember

seeing any hummingbirds fly by." She paused, and then said, 'Wait, maybe just one little baby bird flew by."

I reminded her of our conversation in the car with Dad and at that moment I could see the calm deep breath of relief exhale from my Mom's body. Her solemn face turned into a smirky smile, she had to hurry inside to ask my sister if it was true... "Is there really poop on my jacket?"

My sister replied, with "EWHH! Yes! At least it's little, let me help you wipe it off."

Mom and I looked at each other, started to smile, and both simultaneously said, "It's all good... it's a sign from Dad." At that moment, we both knew he is okay, and we would be, too.

Fortunately, after the little poop incident, my mom's entire demeanor changed. She seemed so much more relaxed and at peace with the whole thing. She told me that she wasn't even really able to cry anymore. I admired her strength, she received her sign and all was content and at peace in her mind. Some people take days, months, or even years to get over death... Mom, with a small sign was able to release the sadness immediately and turn it into something positive. Some others might look at it as lack of emotion, or not caring. But, Mom and I both knew... from the car ride, from our earlier conversations, and from everything we were taught to believe in, that Dad, up in heaven, helped send

One of the hardest decisions you'll ever face in life is choosing whether to walk away or try harder.

us sign from God, that he was okay. And deep down, she truly believed she was going to be fine.

That day, the relationship between my mom and I changed for the better. We seemed to be better able to talk to one another without screaming. She started to show her appreciation for me sticking around and helping her take care of my dad. In fact, she really for the first time seemed like she would be there for me to show me her support. Of course, occasionally we would both regress back into the past... her treating me like one of her learning disabled students and talking down to me like a child... and I would (a little more graciously) remind her that I'm not a kid and please don't talk to me like I'm a 12 year old.

As we worked on putting our lives back together a little more each day, I would hear her on the phone with her sister and her mother. These conversations, too, always managed to turn into a screaming match. Judgments, accusations, hurtful words, which generally resulted in tears and the final huge sigh after the slamming receiver hit its base. Words like "You Can't", "You Shouldn't", "I wouldn't want you to..." condescending, negative words would ring through my head for hours after listening to her phone calls... I even started noticing a trend... my younger sister, now married with a family of her own, when talking to my mom on the phone they tend to get into the same verbally abusive patterns... screaming, judging, crying and getting all worked up.

When you truly don't care what anyone thinks of you, you have reached a dangerously awesome level of freedom.

How do we break these patterns? I have learned that it's really through communication, asking questions and understanding how the OTHER person needs to be communicated with. Learning NLP was a game changer and has helped tremendously with communicating with other people.

It wasn't until much later in life when Mom and I started really talking about how screwed up I thought I had become. She eventually explained how my dad was a little insecure and needed so much to be loved by me, so she helped to create the Daddy's little girl role and pushed me towards him so he would become the parent I would go to for comfort, advice and support.

To this day, I still feel I may never be a priority to my mom. Whether initially it was to encourage my dad, or over time when she became jealous of our close relationship, Mom would and continues to put everything and everyone else first and in my mind I still feel that I will never "Be Enough" for her. Enough of what, you may ask... enough of anything... anything she had hoped or dreamed I would be. I feel as if nothing that I do is good enough, my choices are a disappointment to her, and if there was ever a list of priorities, unless I put on the Jewish guilt, I would most likely be at the bottom of the list. If she doesn't have a class, have to go shopping, wants to make dinner plans, go to a concert, show, play, or just go on a date with her boyfriend, she won't have time to call me back, make

I don't chase after people anymore. If they like spending time with me, they will do so. If not, I'm content with my own company.

plans, and I feel that if an emergency would come up, she may eventually get back to respond a few days later... I know I would have to call someone else if anything needed immediate attention.

What do you do when you feel like there is no one in the world who has your back? Not your parents, not your siblings, not your friends, no significant other... who do you turn to? A religious organization? A networking group?

Really... Do you think anyone with their own lives, their own family, and their own drama would drop anything for me? I felt completely alone, useless and unworthy.

Things almost immediately started picking up for my mom. Invitations with friends, gettogethers with neighbors, before you knew it, she was getting texts and being asked out on dates from men she was meeting online.

The second things started to look positive, we got the call from my aunt. My maternal grandmother had just passed away. Now she was no spring chicken, she was in her late 90s and my aunt and her family were living with her in the home my mom grew up in. I used to stay with my grandma for weeks at a time when I worked in advertising and had a few freelance clients on Wilshire Boulevard in Los Angeles. As she grew older her memory started to deteriorate. I would come to her house after a long day at work and the front door would

Before you give up, thing of the reason you held on for so long.

be left open, the water left running or the stove on with nothing cooking. I was worried about her, but as soon as my aunt moved in, I knew she was under good care.

Then of course, the family claws started to come out. My uncle, a retired appraiser decided that since he had kept his real estate license he would be in charge of selling the house. Now, here I am a Real Estate Broker licensed in both California and Nevada, having tons of great reviews from trusted clients... and my uncle decided first, that he was going to hire a local agent instead of me to handle the marketing of the property and then decided to list it himself.

I looked up the land value, what the recent comps had sold for, and before you knew it, my uncle and his friendly agent had decided to give the house away. I tried to convince them to listen to me for a moment, or at least get a second opinion. All my documents supported a certain amount, and my uncle decided to list it at more than $500 thousand, maybe even more than $600 thousand under market value. He wanted a quick sale to purchase a new home for his family. Now I understand he wasn't intentionally trying to hurt himself, his family, my mom and our family, but this decision did not benefit anyone. The day we all came to clear out all of Grandma's belongings, he said some nasty words, comments and basically told me I didn't know what the hell I was doing and told me to go to hell... I said, "I guess I'll see you there," knowing he would most certainly die before me. And those were the last words spoken between the two of us since that day. He ended up sabotaging my entire family and himself. Knowing the industry and comps, and the market... and even after that transaction was long completed, I still held on to my original opinion that he gave the property away and just because he didn't know any better.

What do you think someone should make on a flipped property? $50, $60, $70, $80 thousand? That lucky individual who purchased my grandma's house from my uncle, was almost as lucky at the investor who got that great deal from the bank that accidentally sold my condo. This investor got Grandma's house at an incredibly crazy low, under market price, fixed it up, resold it, and made over a $900,000 profit. (Yes! over 900 thousand) It just makes my blood boil with irritation every time I think about it. I know... as my friends and family say... "Then just don't think about it."

I try not to, and then again, every time he comes up in a conversation, how can I not? It's like telling someone not to think of the pink elephant... then that's all they can think of. It just blows my mind knowing I could have handed our entire family an extra four, five, or even six hundred thousand dollars more. But, I guess, when someone is so headstrong he can't realize money was dangling right in front of him, there was nothing I could really do... He refused to even listen or give me an opportunity to prove myself.

A million men can tell a woman she is beautiful, but the only time she'll listen is when it's said by the man she loves.

The problem I had, was that half that money could have gone to my mother. She was my priority now that Dad was gone and I felt totally responsible for her financial well being. Unfortunately, there was nothing that I could have done to help that stubborn old man see reality from my perspective. Arghhh.

My frustrations just grew as I remembered one of the many secrets my dad asked me to keep, and one of the responsibilities I had. He said, "I've loaned them (my uncle and his family) thousands and thousands of dollars, that they have yet to pay back. I trust you to look out for your mom when I'm gone and when the time comes, I believe he will do the right thing and give the money back."

"How much?" I asked.

"Too much," he replied. "I should have learned my lesson by now, a few hundred here, a few hundred there, but this time it was a lot more." Then he paused and said, "But he assured me that he will return it."

It wasn't until many months later when my dad revealed the total amount owed. We discussed that he wanted to get the money back. But, my uncle was a little sick, and Dad figured the timing was not right. He mentioned it would be pretty easy during or after the sale of Grandma's house. I just think my dad thought he would still be around to get his loan returned.

More stuff was moved into storage... the storage unit was so full, it was overflowing with stuff... Dad's stuff, my stuff, Grandma's stuff, Mom's stuff. It was definitely time to start dumping. We would go over to the unit, open the door, and just sigh. The sight of it was SO overwhelming from floor to ceiling, with no way in and no way out, without unpacking the entire unit. We would just stand in front of the unit, shaking our heads, we may have found a hat, or a box up front that I could utilize. But, just standing there in front of this huge pile of what used to be my house was just another reminder of how angry and frustrated I was at the bank. We would close the unit door and I would go back to call the attorneys.

As weeks turned into months, and months turned into years, I called and called the attorneys to see what progress was being made, while each time I headed over to the courthouse, I requested documents and paid extra for transcripts. I read and skimmed through hundreds if not thousands of pages and found out that they had missed deadlines, forgot to show up for court dates, and submitted incorrect paperwork.

The attorneys I had believed in and put my life, my house, and my case into their hands had screwed up time and time again... as I continued to pay and get taken advantage of. I was infuriated. I was livid. I would go over to the attorneys office and they would act as if I didn't know what I was talking about. I went to the courthouse and ordered all my transcripts and case files;

Your story could be the key that unlocks someone else's prison. Don't be afraid to share it.

all the attorneys wanted was more money.

I was now going on five years living with my mom out of an overnight bag. Living with my mother in my 40s was already tough, but, then the day came when the judge completely dismissed my case altogether... What? How can they do that?

At this point I was talking to myself...

The bank admitted fault. The attorneys promised I'd have my house back and lots of money or homes in damages... what is this the judge thinking? I didn't ask for this. My slightly hopeful attitude turned into total disappointment. I expected these attorneys to do the job I paid them to do. I interviewed so many. How could I be so stupid as to choose the wrong ones. Should I have seen a sign? My judgement is horrible...

I went deeper and deeper into a depression and true rage against the bank. I blamed myself for not knowing they couldn't or wouldn't do a good job. I didn't understand why these things were happening to me. I drove back over to the courthouse to see why the judge ruled in favor of the bank. Then, it was all clear as day. My attorney had screwed up SO badly, that the judge did not even know how to proceed. I brought the documents over to the attorneys' office and started to scream in hysterics.

A true fiend accepts you who you are, but also helps you to become who you should be.

"Unbelievable!! How could you let this happen? Who are you having work on my case? What the HELL is going on?" I showed them the documents that showed my representative filed the incorrect documents, let deadlines pass, didn't respond to the bank or judge in a timely manner... the judge had no option but to dismiss my case.

"We will file for an Appeal," my attorney muttered under his breath.

I screamed, "You better!"

What good is filing an appeal going to do aside from we get to start over and they get more money to screw up my case all over again. I threatened malpractice.

When I got home I called over 25 different malpractice law firms. Unfortunately, my attorneys, being the so called "the best in the county," were also president of the Bar Association, drank beer, and played golf with all the other malpractice attorneys I called. Not one felt they wanted to go after him regardless of how incompetent his team was. No one would take my case even when I showed them my attorneys filed a "Declaration of Fault" with the court in order to get my case appealed.

I finally did get a referral to a new firm that was willing to settle with the bank if I won the appeal. Of course I won the appeal. Unfortunately, the settlement was for less money than I had even spent on the original

Don't be afraid to get back up again, to try again, to love again, to live again and to dream again. Don't let a hard lesson harden your heart.

attorney fees for their first few months of services!

Goes to show you (or I just proved to myself again my limiting beliefs were correct, and I continued to attract more of the same), "Everyone will take advantage of you if they can."

Why would NO ONE after reading this declaration of Fault file (https://bit.ly/2IO9BoN) take my case? I had lost my home, due to an "OOPS!" from the bank. I had lost my case against the bank due to no one wanting to protect justice and go after a malpracticing attorney. I had lost my home, my pride, my savings, my equity, my 285 gallon saltwater aquarium with all my little fishes and my favorite eel. I hadn't been able to access any of my belongings for over five years after a promise of just, "throw it in storage, you'll be back home in two months, spend as much as possible and you will get it back in triple of the amount with damages since the bank screwed up so badly"...

All I could think to myself is

WHY?... The bank screwed up so badly, the attorneys screwed up so badly, why am I the one that has to bend over and take it? I am just sick to my stomach. I can't even breathe. I don't know what to do, what do I want to do? How and why have I gotten to this point in my life? I am SO angry, bitter, mad, sad, hateful. I can't count on anyone. I can't even count on myself to make the right decision. I failed with working it out with the bank. I failed interviewing the best attorneys. I failed as a roommate and should have been there sooner. I can't trust anyone, not even myself.

I was just a mess. I started to understand why people go postal, why there are suicides, why murder and homicides take place.

Why me? I didn't feel I treated anyone badly, was it a past life I had to make up for? Was this karma coming back? Please God, give me a sign that I deserve this or that it will stop. I thought back... do I remember breaking a little pocket mirror and this is seven years of bad luck... is this just bad luck or is this torture?

What was I living for? What was I going to do now? I didn't know... Actually, at this point in my life...

I didn't even care.

The strongest people I've met have not been given an easier life. They've learned to create the strength and happiness from dark places. ~ Kristen Butler

Character cannot be developed in ease and quiet.
Only through experience of trial and suffering
can the soul be strengthened,
vision cleared, ambition inspired and
success achieved.
It is in the most trying times that
our real character is shaped and revealed.

~ Helen Keller

Chapter 08

~Reflections From The Bottom~

That morning came. That particular morning. That final morning when I laid in bed, paralyzed with apathy, that all I could do is continue to try and justify my own reality. Why should I try to meet the man of my dreams, when he can just turn around and either lie to my face (experience from Dad and previous boyfriends), betray me (experience from Rick), or die on me (experience from my roommate)?

Why should I get up and work to make money and buy a house, when the things I earn and work for can just be taken away (stolen by a boyfriend or taken by the bank)? What is my purpose? Why should I get up and work so hard, just to be pushed aside and not even acknowledged for all the hard work I've done (cheerleading)?

Life is not fair. I know, it's not supposed to be fair, no one ever said that it would be fair. But, I had a really hard time accepting that. Why do some people get the silver spoon and have all the luck? Why do things seem to come so easy to some people? I've tried posting affirmations, going to those motivational talks, read positive self help books, been in and out of counseling for longer than I can remember.

I truly believed down in the depth of my soul that everyone will take advantage and step on me to get ahead, I just can't trust anyone... not my friends, not my family, at this point... not even myself. It seemed like even my past decisions regarding my future and who I could and couldn't trust, believe in, rely on had all steered me in the wrong direction and left me hanging on a very thin string or very disappointed. Were my expectations of people too high, were my expectations of myself too high? I trusted no one, believed in nothing, and in fact, didn't care about anyone or anything either. WOW! That was an eye opening expression of my own reality.

As young kids growing up, my sister and I, when we couldn't sleep, had nightmares, or were scared and went running into Mom and Dad's room. My mom would get up and give us either a vitamin C, (this was to make us strong at night to fight off the bad guys in our dreams) or one little M&M's candy, (this was to ensure we had "sweet" dreams). Mom was smart, that always worked.

Now, years later I think I was looking for that magic "happy pill". The counselors had put me on anti-depressants, friends and family just shook their heads and would say, "Wow, you sure have run into some bad luck." Was it bad luck, or was is just a bad attitude?

When a man truly loves a woman she becomes his weakness. When a woman truly loves a man he becomes her strength. This is called...Exchange of Power

They say when life gives you lemons, make lemonade. How could I wake up and be happy and positive when I couldn't find an ounce of passion or purpose in my blood?

My mind and body were ready to give up. I had stopped caring about others and especially myself. Days went by and I continued to escape into my own dream world wishing it was my reality. I'd get up, go to the bathroom, occasionally shower, grab a bite of whatever was in the fridge and retreat back under my covers where it was safe. Safe from others who in my mind were programmed to sabotage me. Safe from those who wanted to steal, lie, hurt or betray me. I just remember waking up IN my dreams to the most beautiful sunsets over the ocean, looking over a balcony at my sexy husband blowing me kisses while he threw the ball to our dog or into the ocean for him to go fetch. My dream life was magical, no stress, no fighting, no lies, betrayal... exactly the opposite of my reality.

In my dreams I felt so safe with who I was, and I knew the meaning of my existence. I felt relaxed, wonderful, surrounded by positive energies, my mind understood the deep connection to the universe, knowing all answers, solutions to all questions. Always positive, always to my benefit, filled with abundance. I felt confident, nurtured and supported with unconditional love all around me.

Never forget 3 types of people in your life: 1) Who helped you in your difficult times 2) Who left you in your difficult times 3) Who put you in difficult times

"Hey, Liana," Mom would shout, "are you still in bed? You gotta get up and do something with yourself."

"What?" I'd ask.

She would come up with anything... any answer she thought might get me motivated, and I would always answer with, "But, why? Nothing that I do matters," as I pulled the covers over my head, closed my eyes and tried to go back to sleep.

"Do I need to kick you out of my house?" was her final comment, before the tears came pouring from my eyes.

"Please DO!" I screamed... "All I need is one more reason to go park myself and lay down next to Dad and never get up. Go ahead, give me that reason. If you kick me out, not only will I never come back, that will be the end, the end of this pathetic, meaningless, passionless, existence." That was it. I had hit bottom.

That day... honestly I don't remember if it was day or night, I prayed that she would give me a reason to end it... at least I felt with a roof over my head, I could sleep and imagine what it would be like to be dead... never waking up... if I could only go to sleep in this paradise and keep that dream going on for infinity. That's what deep down I started to believe, or at least hoped and prayed that heaven really was.

Then my thoughts started to change and I started to question. If the purpose of living a good life is to go

There are some people who always seem angry and continuously look for conflict. Walk away; the battle they are fighting isn't with you, it is with themselves.

130

to heaven, why didn't everyone just kill themselves as children when they were all young, happy, free, and hadn't committed any harm, lies, or betrayed others? I would think the moment things got really bad, why not get to heaven quick and get this dreary life over with, move on to the next, the bigger, the better, the peace and tranquility of heaven?

OKAY, now I had a better understanding of why suicide really was a way out. The only people who are NOT happy with life and their decision are the people who are stuck in this crummy existence. If they wanted to be at peace, they would join their loved ones in heaven. Why do people stick around if they are so miserable? I laid there and thought of how I would do it. Lots of options came to mind and only one really stuck. I knew exactly how I was going to end my life, if Mom really did decide to kick me out.

Being happy doesn't mean that everything is perfect. It means that you've decided to look beyond the imperfections.

When I was 5 years old my mother always told me
that happiness was the key to life.
When I went to school, they asked me what I
wanted to be when I grew up.
I wrote down "happy". They told me I didn't
understand the assignment,
and I told them they didn't understand life.

~ John Lennon

Chapter 09

~Crossroads~

I didn't really WANT to kill myself, I really wanted to understand my purpose and figure out why I was put here. I was told we all have a purpose and challenges that we need to overcome in our life, I just didn't understand why my purpose was to suffer.

I guess I am pretty much... No! my own thoughts cut myself off...I am definitely stuck! The question is how do I get unstuck? I guess I'll continue to ask around and try to search for better answers.

I went online and look up - **How to get unstuck in life. This is what came up in my search.**

1. **Affirmations.** Tell yourself every positive thing you can squeeze out into your brain. Say these statements in the current and positive as if they are now happening. Example of one of mine is: I spring out of bed with joy and excitement.

That was a far stretch for me. It was a huge lie,

and it didn't work. In fact, my mind kept tellling me, "Nope. Bed is the safest place. Stay right here. Don't leave or you will be sorry!"

2. Pray. Get in touch with your higher self, your God, your light source inside from your soul and pray. Ask for guidance of what you want and direction on how to achieve it;

I prayed and meditated every day. It wasn't doing much good.

3. Ask and research guidance or help.

Been there done that. I went to counselors for years and years, and felt they did nothing except help me relive my bad experiences over and over again. I left most of the time feeling worse than when I walked in.

4. Change your attitude, change your life. Learn NLP, Neuro Linguistics Programming. A communication language that reframes negative thoughts at the unconscious level, and reprograms your brain to become more positive.

Was this my solution? Although anyone who knows me would never imagine me ever writing a book, or bragging about something I didn't think could work. At least not if it didn't work for me. We all think we are the one exception. We all think that MY problems or MY

Neurologist claim that every time you resist acting on your anger, you're actually rewiring your brain to be calmer and more loving.

story is worse than yours. And that is exactly how I felt. I believed my horrible experiences not only supersede yours, but, I believed that I couldn't be fixed. (another limiting belief)

But, the truth of the matter is, **WE ALL HAVE OUR STORIES**, our traumas, dramas, experiences that shape us into who we are today. Good, bad, it really, REALLY doesn't matter as long as we can take a step back and disassociate the actual event or experience from the emotions that were felt. The goal is to continue to feel this disassociation to the current day, even WAY after the event has passed. Our association to the negative emotion that we carry around with us, is what we call our baggage.

I felt like I had a lot of baggage. Dr. Joe Dispensa talks about if you don't know how to control your emotional response or reaction to that event in your life and the refractory period lasts for hours or days... that is called a mood. If you keep that same refractory period going on for weeks, or months, that's called a temperament. And if you keep it going on for years on end, that's called a personality trait. Now, at this point I felt my problems and negative emotions had started to define me. I WAS an unlucky, unhappy, miserable person.

I don't remember the exact day or time, I'm not even sure where or why I opened or clicked an email, or a banner advertisement, or something stating that you

Most often, the people who criticize your life are usually the same ones who don't know the price you paid to get where you are today.

can find your purpose and get on your path through something called NLP. I had no idea what this was, Neuro Linguistic Programming. It sounded technical and my negative attitude imagined that they would send me a technical manual that would need to be translated in order for me to understand. To my surprise, there was a class offered fairly close to my mom's house for a very reasonable price. I had absolutely nothing better to do with my days aside from lay in bed, so I thought, WHY NOT? And then immediately signed up. I knew that at least it would give me an excuse to get out of bed and take a shower.

I hesitantly walked alone from the parking lot into this hotel, staring down at the floor afraid to make eye contact with anyone. All alone I walked down the long pathway between hundreds of chairs and spoke to no one just to choose my seat. I sat close to the front so I could see the instructor and the slide presentation. I chose a spot close to the aisle just in case I needed a quick escape.

As Dr. Matt came on stage and started talking about "the chair", our perception of reality and how we all get stuck, his voice resonated with me SO strongly that I felt my eyes fill with tears that slowly dripped down my cheek. While mesmerized for the first 30 minutes or so, I just listened and I thought... Oh my gosh, he gets it!

It was as if he was talking to me personally, I knew I had

Say goodbye to drama, toxic people and self-criticism. Say yes to more happiness, love in your life, and time with good friends.

walked into the right place, the place that might have my answers. The energy in the room radiated positivity. How could my problems affect me for so long that it got me to the point of STUCK. Why didn't I see this coming sooner? What could I have done differently to prevent this from happening? And the big question was, What do I do now?

I looked around the room, there were a lot of mesmerized students, all sort of having a glassy eyed, hypnotized look. I couldn't tell if they were hearing what I was hearing or if I was picking out specific phrases and sentences that made me want to shout out, "That's Me!" "I'm angry!" "I'm in that gray area... I'm stuck!" Was he really going to let us know what we could do about it? I was so excited that I couldn't wait for more and more information.

Dr. Matt's structure for his seminars was SO interesting to me, I just couldn't wait to get to the exercises and start doing it. He would have us partner up with a neighboring student and we would read some pages, do some visualization, or some linguistical brain scatter talking some mumbo jumbo, and poof... many of the issues that other students in the room had, instantaneously disappeared.

But, not mine, I wondered why... was it my partner? Was it my problem? Was it my brain? He moved pretty quickly through each chapter. There was a ton

The two most important days in your life are the day you are born and the day your find out why.

~ Mark Twain

of information to cover, before you knew it, he'd say, "Moving on to the next chapter." Dr. Matt showed by a raise of hands how not everyone in the room had their problem fixed and that was OKAY because... perhaps we were using the wrong tool. He assured us that eventually the correct tools for our specific problem would come to our consciousness and everyone would have this "eye opening experience". Chapter after chapter... three days passed and as I looked around, many students had changed right in front of my eyes. People evolved, grew mentally, emotionally, intellectually, gained higher awareness to the world around them, and had these amazing breakthroughs. As all this was going on, I grew more and more frustrated, I didn't feel any different. I still felt STUCK.

Then he started to talk about MER®. Mental and Emotional Release... The Big Stuff - The Game Changer. This is the tool I had been waiting for. Supposedly it would help to eliminate ANGER, SADNESS, FEAR, HURT, and GUILT. He explained that those were the key negative emotions that get us STUCK in our past. I had never heard of such a thing. If there was really a way to separate these emotions from the actual experiences and change my perception of my own reality... Count Me In!

We learned another tool that was called 'Parts Integration', this is when part of you wants to do or have one thing, and another part of you wants to do or have something else... this causes your conscious mind some confusion so you need to integrate the parts and find the greatest purpose and cause of each part. Ultimately, you will realize they have the same purpose, so you can then make an educated decision or choice in the direction that is best for you and your higher self.

Wow! I was just amazed with how much information was in this class. I did this parts integration on, "Should I spend money for the next class of this Empowerment, or just go directly to one of Dr. Matt's practitioners and have them do a MER® breakthrough on me?" My unconscious and conscious mind kept telling me to do both… For some reason even though both had the same higher purpose of getting better (or unstuck) finding my passion and purpose so I could live a fulfilling life, the two choices didn't seem to integrate for me, but I was supposed to be able to choose.

Nope. I still at that time felt torn, stuck, and still very, very frustrated. I felt this was another tool that wasn't working for me. My expectation was for this tool to help me decide which direction I should take (thinking there would only be one correct answer). But, in reality, I was not asking the question properly. I should have asked my unconscious mind if I should or should not have a personal breakthrough, and another question of should I or shouldn't I take the next level of trainings? In fact, looking back now, "BOTH" was the absolute correct answer!

Success is what happens after you have survived all of your disappointments.

At this point I was trying to convince myself that this seminar wasn't all just talk with a bunch of paid people or "plants" in the room, trying to sucker me into giving them more of my money... I didn't even trust my research or my decision making abilities after looking back at my past choices that had led me astray and the most recent attorney fiasco.

This next class was a lot more money. A lot more of my money that I felt I may be being suckered into and taken advantage of. I still felt that these sales people would always take advantage of the weak person, and I knew that weak person was me. Ready to be suckered, betrayed and taken advantage of again.

So, I pulled Dr. Matt aside and questioned my own judgment on what he thought would work better. I think he was convinced that I had some type of secondary gain, meaning that deep down I wanted to stay stuck for some perceived internal or external benefit.

I thought long and hard, and there really wasn't any reason I wanted to just lay in bed and do nothing. I just couldn't find a reason to continue plugging away at the daily grind. I needed to find my passion and my purpose. Dr. Matt convinced me that learning the upcoming tools and techniques would be key to my success and they would all be taught and explained in the next class. And, by taking the next class, I would obtain everything necessary to not only help myself but to also help others if the opportunity came up. So, I agreed since I really had nothing better to do or spend my money on. I signed up for another two weeks of this MER® breakthrough and along with that class, I would learn the tools to become an NLP practitioner.

The next class began and I picked another seat close to the front, this time, feeling a little more positive and actually even more hopeful and excited. I have to admit, although still a little hesitant, I did feel slightly motivated to get into the class and learn these tools that would potentially make me happy again.

I recognized a few people and chit chatted with a few new faces. This time an assistant came up on stage and started talking. He kind of bothered me, he talked in a strange pattern as if he was listening to some really bad music and paused in awkward places, it was really hard to follow whatever it was that he was talking about, sounded like a bunch of mumbo jumbo. It didn't make sense and I couldn't consciously process a lot of what he said. I later learned this was a specific linguistical language called the Milton model, a hypnotic way to talk that almost immediately could put you into a trance. At the time, not having this understanding, I was conscious of feeling frustrated while trying to consciously understand what he was saying.

So, I was sitting in this Master NLP class thinking as the awkward phrasing and blah, blah blah sounding

What screws us up most in life is the picture in our head of how it is suppose to be.

monologue was going on upon the stage. My mind again started to wander.

When did things in my life change and go astray? Why and when did I become so pessimistic?

Deeper thoughts (perhaps I was also going deeper into hypnosis) The room was almost in slow motion. It was obviously a gradual change, it didn't happen overnight... or did it?

Was it that one morning when I just didn't want to wake up? Should I have seen that coming and tried to prevent it? I just didn't know.

My mind continued to wander as I thought to myself,

Great, another designation or title to put on my business card. Another thing I really didn't care too much about.

I didn't care because I still didn't believe it really could work. I understood all the physiology and scientific proof behind it working, but I still couldn't understand why these exercises didn't work on me. Dr. Matt would insist it is a "do WITH" not a "do TO" process and the results were the responsibility of the client, not the practitioner. I couldn't blame my partner, I couldn't blame the system or the process, but the only one truly

Every time you get upset, ask yourself if you were to die tomorrow, would it still be worth being upset over...

responsible for making the change or shift in my own perception was myself. I could not be a victim. I had to accept that **I WAS THE CAUSE.**

That was very tough to accept so I said it out loud several times

> *"Okay, so **I'm responsible for my miserable life.** I'm responsible that my cousin attacked me, my dad lied to my face, my roommate lay dead on my living room floor, the bank stole my house, I chose reputable highly qualified attorneys who I CAUSED to screw up my case and made the judge dismiss everything to leave me broke and homeless. Okay, I accept that **I am AT CAUSE and put myself in each of those circumstances and caused those events in my life to happen."***

Then I sighed... a big sigh.

DAMN! Now I felt even worse. **I'm the cause** of my pathetic situation, life isn't fair, people will screw me over, take advantage of me to get ahead, I cannot trust anyone, horrible life.

Well, now I think I went from APATHETIC, to thinking, "Just put a bullet in my head, shoot me like a sick cow, I don't think there is any hope left." I broke down and just cried. I used my quick escape route and walked out of the room with tears pouring down my face.

Moving on doesn't mean forgetting. It means you choose happiness over hurt. Decide to be happy because it's good for your health. ~ Voltaire

I didn't know why I was put on this earth to be the cause of such pain and misery for myself and hoped and prayed to God that I wasn't causing this much pain, deception or discomfort to others. I was a mess. I couldn't go on sitting in that room with all these people having these great breakthroughs, getting over their fears, phobias, transforming from being addicted to licorice or coffee to not having any desire for their vices any longer... right in front of me, transforming their negative habits and beliefs to healthy choices and eliminating negative emotions.

A student who was so angry with a family member and didn't talk to them in years, walked out of the room on a break and called him up. No bad feelings and made up.

I felt even more pathetic. I was unfixable. I was damaged. An assistant came outside, did some additional hypnotic linguistical talking to my brain that seemed to calm me down and get me back into the learning mode (that was cool, I was excited to learn that linguistical chatter talk, and eventually, I did).

I went back to my seat and continued to listen, watch and still be amazingly impressed by what I was experiencing, watching this transformation happen to the students around me. By the end of the first week I felt a little more empowered. I definitely felt determined that I, too, will eventually be able to overcome my baggage issues, even though I wasn't exactly sure what they all

People change for two reasons: either their minds have been opened or their hearts have been broken.

~ Steven Aitchison

were. I realized and accepted my responsibility for many of my past traumas, but, I still wasn't aware of the lessons that I needed to learn.

Now that is a HUGE thing in NLP and MER®– the lessons that you should have learned from any particular negatively charged emotional event must be applied and learned at a conscious and unconscious level. Disassociation from the event and the lessons learned are the only things that can take away the emotional baggage and limiting beliefs that had manifested during that earlier experience. This concept is SO important to understand, I will repeat it again.

> **DISASSOCIATION FROM THE EVENT AND THE LESSONS LEARNED ARE THE ONLY THINGS THAT CAN TAKE AWAY THE EMOTIONAL BAGGAGE AND LIMITING BELIEFS THAT HAD MANIFESTED DURING THAT EARLIER EXPERIENCE.**

I was absolutely determined to breakthrough and become a success story. I tried SO hard to suck up as much information as possible, read all the assignments, learned the scripts, and even practiced in the mirror.

I was definitely motivated and on a mission to gain clarity, purpose, and find my passion.

Dr. Matt suggests that we are like onions. Layers and layers of stuff that just needs to be peeled away to expose

You wouldn't worry so much about what others think of you if you realized how seldom they do.

~ Eleanor Roosevelt

our true selves. I read, I studied, I listened. He told us we will be picking a person in class to work with on this so called amazing breakthrough. I already knew who I wanted to work with. This one girl seemed SO put together, I wasn't even sure why she was there in class. She already had a great practice, experience, and had successfully completed all of her exercises in class that she did with other students. All the students she had worked with experienced excellent results. I approached her at break and was thrilled she had agreed and was excited to work with me.

I was definitely looking forward to the two full days of utilizing the tools, techniques, and mind jumble we had learned. I expected that I would soon become a new, free, happy person, with new goals and a purpose. I couldn't wait. I would be a practitioner first because I was ready, I was ready to utilize all the tools I had learned and help my partner become the person she wanted to be! We started with the personal history, and I immediately saw some language patterns that I could fix, and some limiting beliefs, that I could help her to eliminate. All in all, I think my partner was pretty well on top of things. I thought this would be easy. I believe I had identified her greater (or what we like to call the GREATEST) problem. We went through some linguistic adjustments which worked exactly as we were told they would work.

If you can't do anything about it then let it go. Don't be a prisoner to the things you can't change.
~ Tony Caskins

Then we started the process of MER®:

1. *We investigated and elicited her timeline.*

2. *Determined if she was in time or through time.*

3. *Obtained permission to eliminate the negative emotions.*

4. *Found the root cause.*

5. *Floated higher up and further back–all the way back into her timeline to that specific problematic event.*

6. *Disassociated herself from the actual event.*

7. *Learned the lesson that would serve her better than holding onto that negative emotion.*

8. *Realigned all the events with different choices.*

9. *Floated above her timeline all the way back to now.*

10. *Tested and Future Paced... And Voila...*

"No more negative emotions..."

"Really?" I asked.

"Yes. Really," She stated with a big smile.

We did the same technique for limiting beliefs, and Voila, she felt good, she felt free. We reassessed her values, came up with S.M.A.R.T. Goals. I gave her a

Beautiful things happen when you clear your life of negativity.

homework assignment and she hugged me, took a deep breath, and sighed a sigh of relief... We were both off to a good night's sleep and in the morning it was my turn to be freed from my past.

The morning couldn't come soon enough. I sat in the chair with my box of tissues and waited for my partner, now practitioner, to arrive. She started to ask me about my problem... my list went on and on. She took notes, and continued asking questions. She said she thought she found the greatest problem and would help me to eliminate it.

We went through various tools and techniques and I wasn't feeling any different, why wasn't this working for me? What was I holding back? What wasn't I ALLOWING to happen? I closed my eyes and tried to just flow with the process... I did the visualization techniques, I listened to the linguistical hypnotic language and subconscious phrases, and again to my disappointment I was feeling stuck. I thought my biggest problem was trust and trusting others along with trusting myself, and my master practitioner thought my greatest problem was that I believed 'Life's not Fair'. I agree that was one of my limiting beliefs, but I was not sure if it was "the greatest" problem. Perhaps it was. All I know is that I needed to get rid of it.

Then, to my surprise, she continued to try and explain to me how 'Life really isn't fair' and that I have to accept it.

The only people I owe my loyalty to, are those who never made me question theirs.

She even tried to justify my limiting belief by stating that she tells her daughter that life isn't fair all the time... and we both just have to "deal with it".

Oops! She fell into my perception of reality. If my problem is her reality, there is no way for her to eliminate my belief. She is justifying my negative belief and reinforcing it as a true fact. **If, "Life ISN'T Fair" was my biggest problem and limiting belief, it was HER JOB to convince me that "Life IS Fair" and that my unfair view of the world was incorrect...** Now I knew we were in trouble and we were both now really stuck. We went through the process of MER® across my timeline to when Rick attacked me. Yes! I'm ANGRY. Even when I disassociate myself I was ANGRY! Could I forgive him? NO. Was it hurting me to hold on to my anger? I didn't think I would continue to be angry if I continued to avoid him. I didn't think I would ever be able to forgive him. She was trying to tell me that forgiving him was NOT saying that it was ok for him to do what he did... and my mind could not grasp that.

Was I ANGRY at THIS particular moment? Yes. Would I be ok if he tried it again? NO.

Do I forgive him? NO... what lesson can I learn from being betrayed by a cousin who was like a brother?

All I could come up with was, "Don't Trust Anyone." Friends or family, they will all step on you, take advantage of you, and when you need to count on them they may let you down...

For some reason, I thought this breakthrough was just reinforcing many of my limiting beliefs. Well, maybe not. I didn't feel just ANGER with Rick anymore, I felt INFURIATED, above and beyond anger. I felt DISAPPOINTED, BETRAYED, and absolutely FRUSTRATED... I tried to let go of the Victim mentality, I tried to take personal responsibility and be "AT CAUSE" for my emotions regarding this attack... I tried to figure out what lesson I was meant to learn. And I replayed that day over and over in my head... from going over to help a cousin, leaving when the situation got weird, and what God was trying to teach me, by putting myself into this situation.

Now I just felt drained and depleted. She said, "GREAT! Let's get rid of your Frustration. Right after we get rid of Sadness, Fear, Hurt, and Guilt."

At this point I went through the motions feeling discouraged and exasperated. I was ready to give up and go back to bed. My emotions weren't changing, I was not feeling any sense of relief, or empowerment, or purpose. I was just feeling like a failure that I couldn't even help a competent practitioner help me, help myself. What a loser. Maybe I was meant to be miserable. I tried to talk to an assistant, but as a client, we were told to just go through the process and only the practitioner could ask questions.

If you allow people to make more withdrawals than deposits in your life, you will be out of balance and in the negative. Know when to close the account.

We continued for several more hours to go through the process, one tool after the other, letting her practice each of the tools she had learned on me. And then there was me, stuck in my own frustration of baggage, not knowing how to view the world differently. I was in complete despair. I left the class feeling even worse than even before I started my original NLP training

At least before I was apathetic, now I was in distress. My world was NOT fair (I wasn't able to get fixed, or help myself get fixed), I didn't trust anyone or anything. Dr. Matt said this process would work if I just followed along... I paid good money and got nowhere. I felt taken advantage of, used, and again, definitely in a negative, suicidal frame of mind.

I spoke with Dr. Matt again who still thought I was holding back for some type of secondary gain. He gave me a task and asked me to write down all the benefits of staying miserable and keeping my baggage. And asked, "What will I have to face when it's gone?"

I thought long and hard about his questions and I came up with my answers. I thought at the time that they were pretty lame, and still wasn't sure what he would do with them, but, this is all I could come up with. My answers looked something like this:

One day, you'll just be a memory to some people. Do your best to be a good one.

Benefits of Keeping my Baggage:

1. I can stay single, so there is no need to anticipate fights with a boyfriend or divorce with a husband.

2. I can embrace my independence and never rely on anyone for support or friendship, and thus prevent me from being taken advantage of or betrayed. Continue to be an extreme risk taker, enhancing my opportunity to die and go to heaven sooner. Continue meeting professionals who say they can help me, take my money, and leave disappointed.

What will I have to face if I Let it Go:

1. I will have to find a purpose and do something I like.

2. I will set new goals and look forward to achieving them.

3. I will accept the possibility of being happy again.

4. I will get excited about possibilities and opportunities.

5. I will have the tools to be able to help others with similar issues.

I gave this to Dr. Matt who then pulled a few of the assistants aside and asked them to work with me for a bit during the breaks. He also suggested that I could have access to more qualified practitioners if I attended his Trainers Training Class (another huge out of pocket expense). Again, feeling that I really had nothing better to spend my money on I had another choice, spending my money on a private breakthrough session or take another class that would give me access to a bunch of people who may be able to help me resolve my issues. I was definitely... Yes, still torn, part of me wanted to grow and learn more, and part of me just wanted to have the breakthrough, feel better, and move on. Not knowing what to do, I opted to move on and better my learnings of the process.

After several MER® sessions working with one of the assistants after class, I made a small breakthrough! He used a phobia technique to eliminate my ANGER regarding Rick and another event not mentioned in this book that transpired over 30 years ago.

As he ran the Phobia Model Technique (also used for PTSD) over and over again, I tried to disassociate my feelings and emotions from the actual event that occurred. **(Don't try this on your own - have a licensed practitioner guide you through the process).**

This is **NOT** used for Extreme Fear.

TO LEARN ABOUT MER® OR IF YOU ARE THINKING
ABOUT BECOMING A LICENSED MER® PRACTITIONER,
GO TO:

Website: www.LetitGO-MER.com/MER to learn all the details, understand the instructions, sign up for classes or request a personal breakthrough.

Thanks to the people that walked into my life and made it better. And thanks to the other ones that walked out and made it amazing.

1. *Establish a resource anchor (*<u>learned in class</u>*).*

2. *Utilize the Logical Levels of Therapy (*<u>learned in class</u>*) as a slow build up. When the root cause is so gigantic that you cannot get past it in your timeline, you need to blow out the boundaries (*<u>learned in class</u>*).*

3. *Go back in your timeline to the first event - the root cause.*

4. *Create a movie theater in your mind. The first event will be playing on the screen above your timeline. YOU are running the projector from high above in the projector booth. While running the projector, you are also watching yourself in the audience while watching the movie. This creates the double disassociation from the event and the emotion.*

5. *Run the movie forward in Black and White until the end of the event.*

6. *Freeze the frame at the end and have it turn to black (or white) out.*

7. *Now you are an actor "IN" the same movie, looking through your own eyes. Associate into the memory and run the movie BACKWARDS in color all the way to the beginning.*

8. *Repeat* **(WITH A PRACTITIONER)** *until you cannot get the physical kinesthetic feeling back.*

9. Come back to now.

10. Test and future pace (<u>learned in class</u>)

Okay... My anger was gone. I felt a HUGE weight taken off my shoulders, almost like I could breathe again. WOW! I felt lighter, freer, even a little confused since there seemed to be an empty spot in my mind. He worked with me for hours, going through different techniques.

One by one, Milton Model, Swish Patterns, Parts Integration, hypnosis, Regression, and MER, getting rid of a layer of SADNESS, FEAR, HURT, and GUILT... Yet, even after this breakthrough, I didn't have the hate and anger about Rick anymore, so I couldn't understand why I still felt so lost and STUCK.

I asked my new friend and master practitioner, "Why does this work on everyone else, except me?"

I felt so messed up, I couldn't understand what it would take for me to help myself feel better. We talked and talked until very late in the evening and we came to terms with the fact I had very deep rooted limiting beliefs... I didn't know where they came from or how to get rid of them. I kept meeting with him and other assistants to see if we could make any additional progress.

You can't change your situation, the only thing you can change is how you chose to deal with it.

Transformation is not five minutes from now;
It's a present activity.
In this moment you can make a different choice,
and it's these small choices and successes
that build up over time to help cultivate
a healthy self-image and self-esteem.

~ Jullian Michaels

Chapter 10

~My A'HA Moment~

For the past two weeks I had continued working with different practitioner assistants that were doing their best to help me overcome my baggage and guide me in the release of my negative emotions and limiting beliefs. I had been taking a very stressful yet amazing class (I highly recommend it) called Trainers Training. This is for anyone who wants to present or speak in front of people. It is designed to bring up even more of our baggage and issues. It's the third class in the series - now that we would have the tools to overcome all our own "STUFF", ywe could peel ourselves like an onion, and get to the root cause and disassociate. I prefer to call myself an artichoke instead of an onion... since we all have a big heart in our center, and can now become the best possible presenter that we can be.

Now, as far as I was concerned, I didn't want to be a presenter, I didn't want to train people and certify them to become NLP practitioners or Master Practitioners, I just really wanted to get rid of my baggage and find my own passion and purpose that I had somehow lost over the years. I wanted to find a deep meaningful reason that would inspire me to get out of bed in the morning. I really didn't care about what to do if I got ignored and/ or "BOO'd" off of a big stage in front of hundreds or thousands of people. I had reached the last two days of class when we were supposed to do a huge presentation and conduct an exercise in front of the class to prove we understood the tools, concepts, metaphors, anchors, and all of the other elements that were taught to us over the past two weeks.

Again, I pulled Dr. Matt aside, and stated my disappointment... this time more with myself. I wanted him to utilize his tools from "HUNA": Hawaiian energies to zap me into shape. With all the energy work he does, I just really wanted him to suck out all my negativity and make me feel normal. I couldn't understand why, after all this time, did I still have the limiting belief that 'Life isn't Fair'? So I asked, "Why don't I trust anyone? Why especially don't I even have the ability to trust myself or the decisions I have to make?" I researched and decided to continue this NLP education thinking it would really be able to help me. I let him know that I started to feel taken advantage of AGAIN and in my mind it continued to justify and reinforce my limiting beliefs...

OK, I'll take credit and be at cause, I thought when I walked into the door that "life isn't fair", the sales team will probably try to sell me something I don't need. I anticipated that they would take my money and take advantage of my naive desire to get better... Life really does suck and I feel like I am still the sucker!

Dr. Matt and his congruency with his world around him, Dr. Matt is truly in harmony with his values and teachings. He is congruent and has completely alligned his higher self with his words and his actions. Due to his high ethical lifestyle and business mission, he came to the conclusion that since I didn't feel this particular class was beneficial to or meeting to objective, he offered to connect me with one of his favorite Master Practitioners who was also a Ph.D. in Psychiatry. This doctor was one of his best, and would take the time to work with me individually. I agreed and spoke with Dr. Scott.

This session was different from any therapy session I had ever had. There was a huge difference between other therapists and experts. This doctor explained to me that he didn't need and didn't want to know my story. He told me exactly what was missing from my success and efforts to be happy and positive... to stop attracting negative into my life. The real key had to be: Releasing the negative emotion and limiting beliefs associated with my past traumatic events.

No one, not you or I, can attract what we want by only stating positive affirmations a million times. Especially, if deep down in the depth of our souls, we don't believe anything that we are saying to ourselves is truly possible. Reliving a negative event just embeds the negative

The difference between shool & life: In school you're taught a lesson and then given a test. In life, your given a test that teaches you a lesson. ~ Tom Bodett emotion deeper and deeper into our subconscious mind.

In the past, the more I tried to seek help from therapists, the more I attracted a negative result and then I started reacting exactly in the way of what I was trying to avoid. I continued to become more and more aware that I had become untrustworthy, defiant, inconsiderate. I looked back and noticed I was definitely mean to my mom, critical of my boyfriends, and started flaking out on my friends.

I was becoming the person and taking on traits of the people who had hurt me most and I was trying to avoid. I recognized that I was becoming my dad, my cousin, the bank, the incompetent attorneys. This was my reality. It was who I identified myself with, I wasn't okay.

All I could do was apologize and beg forgiveness from those I loved, cared about and treated poorly. I didn't want to be that bad person, so I did everything I could to reevaluate my words, my actions, and truly ask forgiveness to all those I had hurt along the way. It wasn't until that one particular day when my horribly negative attitude, bad behavior and hurtful comments were really brought to my attention. This was a day that could have been absolutely amazing…until I opened my mouth.

After enjoying a morning of playing in the ocean, a delicious lunch... and then it happened. Not even realizing I had been hurtful to one of the most important people in my life, I carried on with the day as if nothing

Life is not about waiting for the storm to pass but learning to dance in the rain.

I did was wrong. It was my boyfriend, he brought it to my attention in the car on the way home. I listened, I heard what he had to say, I sat quietly for a moment, used some of the tools I had learned in Dr. Matt's class and disassociated myself from the actual event that had just occurred, and realized... Damn!... that really was a mean thing to say. I totally understood why he would be so hurt.

When it came out, I didn't mean it in negative way, it just came out. What was I saying? Why did I say it? Why was I so mean, without even intending to be. All my negative emotions jumbled up from these classes, from my past. I was on a roll trying to discover my true self and who I am, and why I had become the way I am.

I felt horrible! I never intended to hurt this person. I cared for and loved this man deeply. It was so strange, at that moment, I realized I was even more messed up than I originally thought.

While writing this book I thought back and remembered all of those specific details of certain memories that had continued to plague my daily thoughts. I realized how my thoughts and memories had truly affected my unconscious mind and my daily conscious behaviors in the most negative way. I thought about how my unconscious mind had dealt with all those thoughts and negative emotions, and how consciously I was not even aware that they really had NEVER been dealt with at all.

Growth is painful. Change is painful. But nothing is as painful as staying stuck somewhere you don't belong.

How we learn or don't learn to deal with those past negative events and negative emotions is what really matters. How we deal with those emotions and beliefs that have manifested from those past events is the key to breaking free and becoming unstuck. If we are still able to associate into those past events, then the triggers of those negative emotions felt during the event, cannot be released.

I have learned through these NLP classes that the most important key and tool is learning how to disassociate ourselves, separate ourselves from that moment and look at the event as if we are watching a movie and finally being able to see yourself and the event from an outside perspective. Let me repeat that again because this is the KEY to finding your own "A'ha" Moment. This moment will happen as soon as you can learn how and have someone guide you through the process:

> **DISASSOCIATE YOURSELF. SEPARATE YOURSELF FROM THAT EXACT MOMENT AND LOOK INTO THE EVENT AS IF YOU WERE WATCHING A MOVIE. YOU MUST BE ABLE TO SEE YOURSELF AND THE EVENT FROM AN OUTSIDE PERSPECTIVE. ALONG WITH TAKING A STEP BACK IN YOUR TIMELINE TO EVEN 'BEFORE ANY OF THE NEGATIVE FEELINGS THAT THE EVENT CAUSED' HAD BEEN INITIATED.**

Sometimes, in cases of Trauma, PTSD, and extreme Fear (phobias) it is even more important to double disassociate yourself in order to reprogram your unconscious and remove the lingering emotion that you have kept in the forefront of your mind.

My stories are memories of an event that transpired weeks, months and even years ago. Perhaps in a past generation or a previous lifetime. Whether I have remembered these details correctly, incorrectly, the same as my mother, dad, sister, cousin, spouse, neighbor, or friend. The specific details of the conflict, trauma or event 'just don't matter'! Let me say that again, it is very important.

> **The specific details of the conflict, trauma or event JUST DON'T MATTER!**

This is **MY** reality, it's how **I REMEMBER** things taking place, it's how **I FELT** before, during, and after the event. I'm going to speed up my MER® session and go into my timeline and take you to the moment when it all hit me like a ton of bricks. To the moment when I was finally able to release most of my negative beliefs, all of my negative emotions and make room for an incredible positive future.

Whether you believe it or not, whether I believe it or not, something deep down in my unconscious mind, while in a state of hypnosis I was able to bring these various images to the forefront of my conscious mind,

I let go of anger. It helps me to make better decisions and see things more clearly.

learn a lesson, and through the guidance of a master practitioner was able to disassociate far enough from my own experience to release all the negatively charged emotions that I had carried around for what ended up being almost 50 years of my entire life.

Dr. Scott agreed to see me as a patient after class in his Las Vegas office. So, on the last day of class, I hugged my fellow colleagues, other students, the assistants, and Dr. Matt, and left without getting certified as an Official "Trainer" of NLP. This meant that although I was a certified Master Practitioner of NLP & MER®, I would not be able to certify other students or grant them Master Practitioner Status. I flew out to Vegas as soon as Dr. Scott had an opening, and we went through all the steps of the breakthrough process again. He guided me up and over my timeline to my past lives, past generations, and guided me through the process of removing my unwanted negative emotions. After taking all the classes, understanding my real problem and my own personal blockages, I explained to him that I really was not having most of these negative emotions anymore, I was definitely more hung up with a problem of limiting beliefs. I did not know how to get past my issues of TRUST. Trusting others, and especially, trusting myself to make the right choices in my own life.

My greatest problem was exactly what my practitioner thought it was. Not only just 'not trusting' myself and those around me whom I interacted with on a daily or occasional basis, but, also the belief and feeling that **LIFE'S NOT FAIR.** We spent several hours doing this timeline therapy and trying to find the root cause, and I just kept getting stuck. I didn't know why these limiting beliefs would just not disappear. For some reason perhaps my unconscious mind was not ready to let them go. I not only gave it permission, I deeply wanted it to be released. I demanded my higher self to let them go and I started to cry again.

Dr. Scott and I talked for several more hours and he ended up rediagnosing me with several more events that caused the many symptoms of PTSD. We ran the PTSD and PHOBIA model (another NLP tool) over and over on ALL those events and the stories I've mentioned to you in this book. I really kept trying to consciously accept responsibility and learn some type of lesson that perhaps could have prevented my cousin attacking me, for the death of my roommate, for the bank stealing my house, for my father's lies and it just kept coming back to me that **LIFE ISN'T FAIR!** Yes, I know you probably also think that life isn't fair, we have all heard it a million and two times. The difference is, for ME it's a problem - **A HUGE PROBLEM.** For you, it may not be. You may think, yes, sometimes it's fair, sometimes it's not... no big deal, and deal with whatever cards you are dealt. For me, it's an extreme fact of my reality. I, deep down, had the belief (as if it was clear as day and night) that life was not fair to ME. I don't trust people. I don't trust myself.

Dear life, I understand very clearly that you are not fair so you can stop teaching me that lesson.

I have been projecting it out onto the world for as long as I could remember, because that is what and who I continued to attract. I chose men who lie, cheat, steal... I expect to get screwed over and sure enough, I would prove myself correct every time and time again.

Once I thought I had made a mental change, learned my lesson, repeated those positive affirmations thousands of times, watched subliminal videos on how to attract the perfect love into my life, I would then date someone who I had hoped was different. After several years of being together, I felt so strongly that all I truly wanted was his, mine and our happiness. We had so much in common and enjoyed each other's company... there was absolutely no reason why this man was not "The One." I felt it deep down to my core. I wanted to be with this man until I could no longer be on this earth. He meant everything to me, I would do anything for him. And I believed he returned the love and affection equally.

Didn't I deserve to grow old with someone who loves and adores me? Well, apparently, even at this point of my life, a few months prior to hitting the 50 year old mark, it became even clearer that I have been dating the wrong man. Five, six, seven years into our relationship, he informs me of HIS value system and lets me know time and time again that he has absolutely no interest in marriage or family. So, even though I know this man is wrong for me, I had continued to stay and hold onto this dead end relationship.

If you focus on the hurt, you will continue to suffer. If you focus on the lesson, you will continue to grow.
~ FB/Buddha Daily

Why?

We deeply care for each other, enjoy each other mentally, emotionally, and physically. I thought we could be happy together. The problem was that we didn't and still don't want or have the same relationship goals or values as each other.

As each day, week, and month had passed, I would hurt deep down, more and more, not understanding why this perfect man didn't want to be with ME forever. There was a time when he said he wanted to grow old together, but didn't want all the responsibility or commitment that came with it. As this relationship grew, my limiting beliefs grew stronger. I was not his priority and I never would be. I wasn't necessarily always at the bottom of his list, but I came after his home, his job, his animals, and unfortunately, the situation didn't allow for me to become part of what he already had. And he made it perfectly clear, that he didn't want to change his current situation. So, it happened that his daily life just couldn't include me. And once again I continued to doubt my choices.

Is there is such a thing as a healthy relationship when it comes to family, fidelity and security? Why is there so much divorce, is it worth even trying for... or just hang on to whatever good is coming from what I have? I was told this is settling. Am I settling for

If another woman steals your man, there's no better revenge than letting her keep him. Real men can't be stolen.

my true love? I didn't think so. He is/was everything I had always dreamed of. He just didn't want me. Life just isn't FAIR to ME.

Dr. Scott said, "Let's try something." We started to combine a tool called "regression" with the "timeline" therapy, relaxation, and hypnotherapy. I demanded my higher self to bring forward and bring to my conscious the root cause of my limiting beliefs. In my mind, over my timeline I went all the way back to my childhood to when I was still free from worry, no negativity, naive happiness and excitement to try new things and trusted everyone and everything around me.

He brought me back to a time when I was just a kid, somewhere between five and six years old. My sister was just a little baby in a carrier, breast feeding from Mom. We were at a place called Bush Gardens, a big park filled with birds, a lake, landscaped with trees and flowers and walkways with lots of park benches. I could smell the aroma of what I now know as a the scent of a brewery. We fed the ducks and bunnies with the little food you can purchase for a dime, we even went on the little gondola boat, and rode the tram ride around the park. We were spending a lovely weekend morning together as a normal healthy family. The sun was beating down on this hot summer day, I could feel some of the sweat beads dripping down my cheek. I remembered passing a big cart filled with ice and plastic juice containers. I

Forgive yourself for not knowing what you didn't know before you learned it.

could feel the cool water misters blowing toward my face as my dad lifted me up to peek inside, there was a big round orange shaped container filled with orange juice, a yellow shaped pineapple filled with pineapple juice, a red apple filled with apple juice, and purple grapes filled with delicious smelling grape juice. Each one had a tiny green straw and I asked Dad if we could get some. One for him, one for me and one for Mom to share with my baby sister. I thought if I was thirsty everyone might be thirsty. My dad smiled and agreed. I chose the purple grape juice, and Dad chose an apple, and an orange, too.

So excited, Dad took my hand and I skipped back to meet Mom who was nursing my baby sister on one of the benches. She chose apple and Dad had already sucked down most of the orange juice. I squealed with delight getting ready to drink some deliciously cold purple grape juice. I stuck my lips around the green straw and sucked up a few bubbles, and I quickly realized that the straw could barely reach the liquid. "Dad," I said in a sad voice, "my juice is almost empty and I didn't even get to drink it yet. Why didn't I get a full one?"

At that moment, my dad stood up as if he was on a mission... or as I think back now he was probably thinking, "I'll show this vendor a thing or two...," took my hand and we walked quickly away again, as if my skipping was not fast enough, he pulled me away as if I was flying through the air, leaving Mom and my sister to enjoy the tweeting birds and fragrant flowers. While

Don't promise when you're happy. Don't reply when you're angry and don't decide when you're sad.
~ quoteslifedaddy.com

walking briskly back to the juice vendor, my dad looked at me and said, "Liana, I need to teach you how to protect your rights, people will always try to lie, steal, and take advantage of you, or they will step all over you to get ahead. You need to watch out. Life isn't fair, so you need to fight for what you want and what you believe in, and ALWAYS protect your rights." He took a deep breath like he had just revealed the secret of life and how to get what I want. "Do you understand me?" he asked.

"Yes, Dad. Always protect my rights because life's not fair and people will lie and take advantage of me," I repeated with a smile.

We reached the guy at the juice stand and Dad said, "My daughter is unhappy, we would like a new drink, she thinks that somehow it either wasn't filled properly or it was spilled before we purchased it. May we exchange it for a full one?"

"Of course," said the nice man, and he even asked if I wanted to pick out a new one by myself. My dad lifted me back up in his arms, high enough for me to reach up and touch the misters with my fingers. I could feel them blowing the cold mists of water in my hair, and then they produced large droplets, cooling off the sweat that was dripping down my cheeks from the heat of the late morning sun.

I looked around, pointed to another grape juice, one that appeared full, looked up at the nice man and

As I follow the path of forgiveness, life becomes a new, clean slate on which I can draw my new life plan as I wish.

smiled. We thanked the nice man, and walked back to Mom. **Apparently, that WAS the LESSON of MY LIFE.** At around five years old, the man I trusted whole heartedly told me Life wasn't Fair, people will always take advantage and lie to me. OH MY GOSH! That was it! That was the exact moment when and where MY REALITY came from. I had believed it my entire life and it wasn't even my belief... it was my father's belief... *****THAT WAS THE LESSON***** I didn't need to carry it with ME anymore. I could let it go and give it back to where and to whom it belonged. That was the moment I realized that my limiting beliefs were not mine at all. I had that "A'HA" MOMENT of transformation. All the MER® sessions, all the negative emotional release therapy, and all the previous work I had done prior to that moment did not seem to work until... now!

> *All of a sudden everything fell into alignment and I finally feel totally congruent. I now have an understanding where I am and even better, how I got here. I'm feeling an overwhelming calmness and freedom that I don't remember ever having experienced.*

Dr. Scott told me that it would be years before all the levels of my onion were peeled, how other beliefs and emotions would eventually come up and make me aware of some other traumatic event or situation, but not to worry about them UNTIL they, too became a problem. A problem for ME. At this moment, I truly felt that we

I realize that my parents gave their best to me. I forgive them for any wrong that they unknowingly did to me.

had made good progress. I just needed to follow up and continue becoming more selfaware and when serious issues or problems came up, I now had and understood the specific tools that could help me overcome them. For me, (and this may not be necessary for you) it was the lesson that not only needed to be learned in order to let go of any limiting belief or negative emotion, but my conscious mind needed to be fully aware of its lesson and how to implement it in my daily life.

In the classes I took, I was told and accepted that my unconscious was supposed to take me where it needed to go, learn what it needed to learn and I should then feel free. When, in fact, my conscious mind also needed to actually become aware of the lesson, understand and accept the lesson in order to process the information that my unconscious was presenting. Once my conscious mind was in alignment with my unconscious mind, things started to change for me, and they started to change quickly.

That same afternoon we floated up and further back through my timeline, to past lives and past generations. I saw myself through my own eyes killing innocent people, this could have been during the time of war.

I feel like I don't want to be doing this. I remember thinking, but, I have to. It's them or me as I shot and killed those innocent people, people I thought and feel like I know. I had to do it... I had to in order to survive. I shed a tear since it feels like they are people I care deeply about.

So, what was the lesson to be learned there? Survival? People did what they had to do to survive, it's not always by choice, and you have to put yourself first...? Okay, I took that as the lesson. It wasn't betrayal, it was survival.

Another event back in the timeline, I remember walking up to a military person in a room. "It's you and your family, or them. You get to choose," I watched him say as he pointed down into the camp below his office window.

I remembered seeing groups of crying families all huddled together and as they scream and call out with their pleas to let them live, my watch falls off my wrist and I toss it to one of the crying men, who is trying to console his family. Does this give him hope? I don't know. As this family falls to their deaths, I reach down into a pool of blood to pick up my now blood dripping red watch band and observe their little baby choking and drowning in her own parents' blood. I gag, drop the watch, and turn to walk away...

Damn! What lesson is to be learned here?

Was it that bad choices had to be made to save my family? Could I, should I forgive myself? Was it even really me? I can see it

I'm still the same person, I just view things differently now than I did back then.

just like a memory through my own eyes. It feels very real although it doesn't feel like me right now, could it have been an ancestor?

All I know is once my conscious mind was aware of the lesson, I was able to disassociate myself from the event, float higher up and further back, before any of the events that led to that event and release the negative emotion of fear, a belief of betrayal, then I could go back down into the event, see it for what it was, and float back to now without that feeling of betrayal or fear.

It was SO strange. It made me think back to my dad as he would tell me stories in the hospital bed when he came back into consciousness after one of the medically induced comas the doctor would put him in after a chemo treatment. Could this be why he was afraid of drowning? Could that vision be of him drowning in the pool of blood, or could that be the same watch he had dropped in his hallucination while under sedation in the hospital? Could there be any correlation? Did it matter? Did any of these stories, visions, memories matter?

NO!

The beauty of this entire NLP/MER® process is that the specific details of any of our stories just don't matter. No one needs to know the details of what you went through, the specifics of why you are angry, sad, hurt, etc. They just don't matter to anyone except to a psychologist that wants you to relive those traumas over and over again.

Tell me how you feel, what will you do now, or take these medications to feel better. What happens if you don't feel better?

For years and years I had been meeting with traditional therapists and prescribed anti-depressants because of calling off engagements, to filing bankruptcy, through the times when I was lied to, cheated on, and stolen from, and many of life's other unfortunate and unpleasant situations…

Until it all changed. Several months after my MER session, a situation that if it would have happened in the past, would have caused me to be outraged and it would have reinforced my limited beliefs and negative emotions. But, This time my response to this situation was completely different. I was able to utilize the lessons I had learned in my breakthrough and I had finally reinforced in my own mind and felt confident that I could share with others, my "Aha Moment" really and truly worked as they said it would. A new problem that I really had no control over did not effect me the same way it had in the past.

It wasn't until the letter came in the mail from the IRS. The letter stated that the bank claimed my settlement money as 'Other Income' and expected me to pay taxes on it. What? To throw salt in an already open wound. Did receiving this letter affect me in the huge negative way with an angry emotional charge that I had anticipated?

Actually, no. I very calmly put all my documents from the settlement together... all 369 pages, and some legal jargon that stated "a settlement is not taxable income". I faxed it all to the IRS, three, four, maybe five times, filling up their fax machines with itemized proof that I didn't need to pay taxes on my losses.

Did I have an emotional charge? No. Was I infuriated as I used to be regarding my loss? No. Was I annoyed... sure, but really it was more of just an inconvenience. I really did not have an emotional attachment to this event as if they were trying to screw me over. Somehow, that day with Dr. Scott was **the day I was able to Let that and more ALL Go.**

I later described my experience with Dr. Scott to another classmate, now master practitioner. Marina had been a healer for many years, worked with Shamans and is a life coach. She gave me another amazing tool to release all this residual pent up negative baggage.

Baggage is: things, memories, emotions, stuff, or basically anything from the past that you should have let go of, but have not... yet. I will share this process with you. Get into a comfortable location, close your eyes and breathe, focus on your breath.

Now, imagine a large empty field, tell you unconscious

I am currently under construction...Thank you for your patience.

mind to allow all the negativity of your past to float up out of the field in black bags. Allow these bags to keep floating up until they float away. Keep doing this until there are no more black bags.

Now, let me tell you... I originally had a problem with this exercise, too. The black bags got so big and just hovered over the field, they would not disappear, until I imagined them being shot to the point of being blown up and finally exploding. Once these bags had burst, another set would start growing, growing larger and larger until the field was filled again with more of these black bags. This shooting and exploding exercise went on for over four months.

I spent about 30-45 minutes every night as I lay in bed, focusing on my breath and choosing one element of the five quadrants of my life to remove my negative energies from. One at a time, Family, Relationship, Career, Health and Fitness, Spirituality, and Personal Growth/ Development.

I started removing the black bags of my life, everything that needed to be brought to the surface in general to get the flow of release into motion, then it happened. One evening while lying in my bed, fewer and fewer bags grew, they were lighter, they floated up with ease, they floated up higher and higher until they disappeared out of my vision... The next day (mind you this is a process that I worked on daily for many months) there were no

Perfect Maturity is when a person hurts you, and you try to understand their situation & don't hurt them back.

bags... just a field, an empty field.

I wondered, is this possible? Can all of my negative emotions and baggage be gone? I looked around the field and gave myself an even larger view of my surroundings in my mind. They were all gone. All I saw was a dead, blown up, empty field.

After so long, it continued to be my nightly ritual, kind of like brushing my teeth. I would lay down, breathe and start the meditation process, and slowly over a few more weeks, the field turned green. Eventually, little flowers started to bloom, and I felt that I was finally at peace. As I took a deep breath in, and slowly let it out, I knew I was ready to take the next step of my emotional transformation.

Remember my story at the beginning of this book about trying out for the 1984 Olympics? Remember when I was standing there, prepared to perform in the most important audition of my young life? The music played and I danced my heart out. I remembered a girl from the front row got a tap and her smile grew even bigger as she ran to the back table to give her contact information to the Olympic Committee.

Continuing up and down the rows, a tap here, a tap here. The chosen girls were getting giddy, laughing and sighing with relief that they were chosen as they ran to the back table. "Quiet!" the judges yelled. My heart continued to race, it was pounding SO HARD

The meaning of life is to find your gift. The purpose of life is to give it away. ~ Pablo Picasso that I could hardly stay focused and hear the music, so I continued counting the beats in my head as my sweat started to drip into my eyes.

Up and down the rows the judge walked... he went right by me... I could feel the tears wadding up in my eyes. Maybe he'll turn around, maybe he will come back. What was only a few minutes seemed like hours. The music ended... there was only a small group of us left standing in the middle of the room... I looked to the side and recognized that the other girl from my school was left standing there, too. She looked back at me with a sad look in her eye.

Everyone was quiet... as the judge walked around looking if he should pick just one or two more girls... my mind was spinning and my emotions were drowning.

What could I possibly do now? Is there something I should I have done differently? Kicked higher? Smiled bigger... is there anything I could do now to change his mind? I'm not being chosen to go to the back table. Is it because of my lack of support from my friends and my last minute insecurities... Why aren't I good enough?

Well, let me take you back... back to that day as the judge continued to walk up and down the rows of the last few remaining girls. I was not tapped on the shoulder. My heart sank, the deep pounding in my head slowed down,

Everything we hear isan opinion not a fact. Everything we see is a perspective, not a truth.
~ Marcus Aurelius

and my smile slowly faded.

Was I sad? Yes. Was I disappointed? Yes... But, that was a temporary emotional disappointment. Would that be a negative moment that would be ingrained into my brain and last forever?

The judge walked to the front of the room to grab the microphone. The girls in the back were already celebrating and the parents who were peeking through the crack in the back doors were all hugging. Then came the big announcement.

"I want to thank everyone for coming and getting this far. I know it's a very exciting opportunity and we wish we could accept all of you, but we can only take the very best of the best to represent the young women of California to dance and take part in the Opening Ceremonies of the 1984 Olympic Games. We know this will be a memory of a lifetime and we are glad you all chose to come out and participate in the try outs."

As my heart sunk even deeper, he continued to speak.

"Now, ALL the girls in the back of the room, please don't forget to leave your name and number with one of the representatives at the back table, as I'm sure most of you have already done. We will let you know if any additional positions open up".

He paused, took in a deep breath and said, "Congratulations to all the remaining girls in the room, you are officially members of the 1984 Olympic Opening Ceremonies Dance Team!"

My heart about stopped. What did he just say? I thought in my head, Am I hearing him correctly? I was a little shocked and confused. I looked around the room, the representatives at the back table were looking toward us in the center of the room, then they stood up and continued clapping with big smiles.

> *I'm still standing here, my mind is racing. I wasn't tapped on the shoulder, and I thought I wasn't picked... and,* **Oh my gosh, I didn't fail! I made it!** *My repounding heart feels like it's going to explode. My emotions are so up and down, I'm not sure how to react. I can't help my face from smiling ear to ear as my emotions become filled with overwhelming ecstasy!*

This potential disappointment was one of the most positive memories of my life. Something I knew deep down in the depth of my soul that I so passionately wanted to achieve, I had no choice but to be 100% confident and sure of myself.

I wanted and craved that SAME confident feeling of being capable of accomplishing anything back. Where did that passion, excitement, anticipation go?

A little more than 30 years later, I finally understood

God's love is like an ocean; you can see it's beginning, but not its end. ~ Rick Warren where that passion went. It went away, sucked out through other negative experiences and negative emotions hanging and lingering on. Time and time again, I faced other disappointments, traumas, challenges that either I couldn't or didn't want to take responsibility for happening. I had built up so many limiting beliefs and negative emotions, I had become stuck in my own victim mindset. No wonder I couldn't get out of bed and didn't know what to do with myself.

Why doesn't anyone tell you how to release that sadness and disappointment so you can turn around and look at it as just another step or opportunity to get closer to what you really want? How could I look in the mirror and repeat positive affirmations that I am successful and accomplish my goals and dreams when I thought the world was there to step on me, take advantage of me, and will screw me over to get ahead? It took disassociating myself from my own story to allow my unconscious mind to look back at these events as if I was watching a movie.

When you see a trauma in a movie, you feel for the person, you empathize and imagine how you would feel if you went through what they had gone through... but then, you can walk out of the theater, wipe off those tears, and move on.

That's the power of MER® and the tools of NLP. Understanding the prime directives of the unconscious

Don't rush your healing, don't pretend to be okay when you're not and don't apologize for being broken.

~ Lizelle Gutierrez

mind, associating and disassociating from a traumatic event that caused a negative emotion or limiting belief. Once we can convince our unconscious minds that we are no longer living IN that horrible moment, we can take the learnings FROM that moment and then choose how we want to feel.

Take responsibility or be **"AT CAUSE" of our current emotional state**. We call this emotional intelligence[8]. We can no longer play victim, we must be A**t Cause, Learn our lessons and then Decide how we want our lives to play out**. Only I have the power to affect my life, my beliefs, emotions and my perceptions. It's amazing how once you learn the tools, you can change the way you think and feel and having that control gives you Empowerment. Again, another take home if you are looking for key points from this book...

Once you learn the tools to release your unwanted negative emotions, you can change the way you think and feel. Having that control gives you Empowerment!

Being EMPOWERED allows you to live the life that you had always wanted, and didn't know how to achieve.

Always remember, if you have been diagnosed with PTSD, it is not a sign of weakness; rather, it is proof of your strength, because you have survived! ~ Michel Templet

We must develop and maintain the capacity
to forgive.
He who is devoid of the power to forgive
is devoid of the power to love.
There is some good in the worst of us
and some evil in the best of us.
When we discover this, we are less prone
to hate our enemies.

Martin Luther King, Jr.

Chapter 11

~Hurt &
Forgiveness~

It was Rosh Hashana, the Jewish New Year, and I was 48 years old. I had been trying to make conscious changes in my life, right the wrongs, and be the person God put me on this earth to be. Recently, I was flipping through the news feed on my Facebook and saw a birthday posting for Sara who just turned 14. I couldn't believe how time flew. Now you may ask, who in the heck is Sara? Sara is Chrissy's granddaughter. Jeff 's daughter, the one I promised I would always be there for.

Well let me tell you... Do you have any idea how much emotional baggage (GUILT) I have hung onto for not being there for those two boys, not watching their kids grow up, not sending them holiday cards and gifts over the years.

Oh my gosh, here come the tears. I cry every time I think of how I broke my promise and abandoned those kids and left them with who I felt was an evil monster. I have avoided family events, blocked Facebook pages, and have done everything in my power to put that one hot summer day behind me... and 32 years later it still triggered a negative emotional response.

Ok, now that I had the tools, I wanted to see what could be done. I'd already had several MER® breakthroughs and released my Anger, Sadness, Fear, Hurt, and Guilt the best I could. So, why was I still so upset with tears in my eyes regarding that unfortunate day?

NLP suggests that YOU NEED TO LET GO OF A (a mental limitation) = TO GET B (a shifted mental awareness). See the following chart from Dr. Matt's Empowerment Partnership Class. One Needs to:

LET GO of "A"	to GET "B"
- VICTIM	= UNDERSTANDING
- HURT	= SELF ACCEPTANCE
- GUILT/UNWORTHINESS	= FORGIVENESS
- CONTROL	= PEACE, FAITH, TRUST

The above were my main issues

It may not be obvious to you, but to me... it was obviously GUILT.

So, as Dr. Scott, Mariana, and Dr. Matt reinforce in their teachings, my onion or artichoke layer had been peeled to expose the next or deeper layer of guilt. This brought up more stuff that needed to be eliminated in order to make room for the positive. Not an easy task at hand, but

I knew it was time. Was it time for me to forgive Rick?

Even after going through all the motions of listening to a CD of Ho'oponopono[9], I still didn't think I was ready to completely let that day go. Not yet, maybe someday. Right now, my emotional problem was guilt, unworthiness, not stepping in and up for the boys.

It was time for the phone call. I didn't even have their phone numbers, all I had was a Facebook profile, good thing there is a Facebook messenger. I sent messages to both Jeff and Dov asking them to call me.

We spoke on the phone and I asked them both for forgiveness, as I told them why I was unable to keep the promises that were in my letter.

Dov, just a toddler at the time, didn't remember the letter, and didn't have much to say. Very military like, direct, and non emotional towards his father. He assured me all was good and we will definitely try to keep in touch and reconnect over the next few years.

Now Jeff, Chrissy's older son, really surprised me. We had such an amazing conversation, that I became teary eyed all over again on the phone. This time not from guilt, but, instead from joy. He not only remembered the letter, but, he brought up HIS memories of the times we spent together before his mother passed. Activities at the beach, lunches at the park, many of the times we had spent together were also all positive in his mind. He said

If you can't be a pencil to write anyone's happiness, then try to be a nice eraser to remove someone's sadness.

so many heartwarming comments about his positive past memories of the times we shared with his mom, how I was like a big sister, and possibly his first crush.

My heart melted as in his perspective, I had never abandoned him like I felt that I had. He felt I was always there, and he told me how much he appreciated after his mom died, while sitting alone, feeling sad, he read my letter and it warmed his heart.

I needed to make a difference and support both him and his brother at that horrible time in time in their lives, and even without knowing it for all those years, until that day on the phone, he communicated that I had. I had made that horrible day for him, just a little better. A little easier, and that was all I ever wanted to do.

Over time, the relationship between both boys and their father had deteriorated almost to the point of no interaction or connection. I was assured that the daughters of both my cousins would not be put in jeopardy or be left alone with him. I was now able to forgive myself, the burden of guilt and abandonment had slightly lifted.

I'm sure as time goes on and I am truly able to understand my lesson from that day, I will be free from reliving it. Although now, I can still go through each detailed moment of that day in my head, I feel okay about it. The vision in my mind is a little like watching a really good tear jerker movie, over and over, I know what's going to happen, I have become desensitized to it, and it doesn't really affect me on a daily life as it used to. It's just an event from my past that no longer has a negative bearing on my future.

Although sometimes the tears still flow, I know as time goes on and I can see with my own eyes that both boys are okay, I may even eventually be able to entirely forgive myself for taking that step back and not intentionally including myself in their growing up events and pivotal points in their lives... In my mind, I just couldn't be there to support them in the way I had hoped or expected that I would.

I just wanted to pick Jeff up through the phone and give him a big hug like when he was a kid. He would run out of the ocean or jump off the swing. I would twirl him around by the arms, and say, "Everything is going to be okay, it all gets better from here." We planned a trip for him to come out to visit within a year or two. I didn't want to wait. I'm hoping I can get out there at least for the book launch and give him a copy.

There is special meditation that I learned in my NLP class that other NLP classes don't offer. My instructor Dr. Matt comes from a long lineage of Hawaiian Teachers who studied the ancient teachings of HUNA - energy work.

Until we have seen someone's darkness, we don't really know who they are. Until we have forgiven someone's darkness we don't really know what love is. ~ Marianne Williamson

There is a wonderful guided meditation called Ho'oponopono, It's the Hawaiian Code of forgiveness.

You can find a shortened version on YouTube by going here:

https://youtu.be/FaMcgtswmVA

(If the link has changed, you can find an update on my website)

There are two original versions, one for daily forgiveness in general, and one for events that took place with a specific person who you may need to forgive. My very favorite meditation actually was done live in one of Dr. Matt's classes. It's when you imagine yourself taking the main role in this meditation, and you alone go up onto a stage - and you are finally able to finally forgive yourself.

Here are a few thought provoking questions for my readers. Take some time and find the real answers:

1. *When was the last time you forgave yourself?*

2. *Do you take responsibility for where you are in life, or are you the victim of circumstance?*

3. *Do people around you cause you or make you feel a certain way?*

4. *Do you blame others for your negative circumstances?*

Once you have grasped the concept that "You are at Cause", you can forgive yourself for not knowing any better. One of my favorite sayings is: "You don't know what you don't know". Once you learn and accept this new knowledge, you can utilize the positive energies, your higher powers, your belief in whatever you believe in and forgive yourself for not becoming aware of this before now.

Teachers of energy also say that when the time is right, the answers will appear. It was that time. Once I cleared out as much negativity as I could (at least the first layer of my artichoke), I continued to learn and meditate, and utilize the tools and techniques to move forward in achieving my goals. I believe that this Ho'oponopono meditation was a game changer for me. So many events came to mind, so many beliefs about my self doubt and my insecurities. I was able to go back into my childhood when I was pure, naive, and innocent and as an adult, and talk to myself when I was a child. I was able to hold my own hand and let myself know that everything will be ok, that this is how I turn out. Asking and being able to forgive myself and let myself know what is to come.

Asking that small child(me) to forgive myself for what I had put that child through was a VERY releasing and Empowering tool.

I truly believe that if you are reading this book, it's for a reason. Perhaps it's time for YOU to take advantage of

I forgive myself for being imperfect like everybody else. However, I still manage to live the best life that I can.

MY research, my stories, and my traumas. Once you, too, have released your negative emotions, limiting beliefs (through MER®) and reevaluated your values, gone back into your timeline - to a time when you were pure, naive, and innocent, and asked yourself for forgiveness and are able to grant it to yourself, I can guarantee that this process will allow you to not only remove your blocks, but make space for the positive by giving yourself the permission to really feel whole again.

I just love the concept of forgiving others for "Not being the (person) I expect and wanted them to be." In the quoted section where I put 'person', you can insert, husband, wife, mother in-law, neighbor, best friend, parent... anything that fits

Another important thing to remember is to: **NOT TAKE ANYTHING TOO PERSONALLY**. We live in a world of survival of the fittest, and most people focus on **WHO?**

THEMSELVES!

Now, when I notice the feeling of hurt begin to arise, I now have the understanding that I am the cause for that hurt. I have the expectation of someone doing, saying, or being something that I wanted them to do, say or be. If I have no expectations for anyone to be anything other than themselves, and have the perception that they are doing the best they can for themselves at that moment, then I can no longer feel hurt. When I see

Everything happens for a reason. Everything leads to something positive.

myself becoming irritated by someone else's actions (or lack of actions), I need to take a step back, recognize my feelings and say out loud, "I forgive YOU for not being the person I expect and want you to Be." Then the chains are broken and I am free to move on.

Yes. We all have a certain expectation of what we want others to do. For example, I felt that the attorneys working for me to get my house back had a certain duty and responsibility to execute their job properly and efficiently. That is why I had agreed to pay them a hefty monthly retainer. When they lacked in their ability to perform their duties, it was MY responsibility to call them on it, not to just trust them. Unfortunately, I was unable to find a competent firm to go after them for malpractice. Even after receiving pages and pages of them admitting their incompetence, I doubted myself in my research and limited myself from acquiring a competent replacement and solution.

So, if you know of, or are a competent Malpractice Attorney, and would be interested in helping me get some justice, please contact me.

I also had a certain expectation with bank employees who clearly stated (I have name, date, and times of specific phone calls), that I was not in default, and had nothing to worry about regarding my home... yet, when MY expectations were not met, I was clearly hurt, frustrated, and wanted to blame everyone else. I needed

There is good to be found in every situation, even if I may not see it at the moment. There is always a solution to my problems.

to forgive those employees for not doing what I expected them to do, for not being ethical, logical, or doing the correct thing... for whatever reason they had, perhaps they were afraid of losing their jobs, not getting their bonus, or just plain didn't care... I needed to forgive them and not take it personally...

Do you know how hard that is to do? **Oh My Gosh!** Not take it personally, losing my home, my equity, my money, my pets... my positive frame of mind... my reality as I once knew it...

Yes! Once I realized, that it's **MY EXPECTATIONS** of people in today's society, I felt a bit relieved. Could I just shift my thinking to that the majority of people really are actually just incompetent? Even though I though to myself, "How sad..." It really did help me to feel better about myself and my personal past choices. Perhaps they actually didn't do it on purpose, maybe they had no intention of taking advantage of me. They (hopefully) just didn't know any better. Alexanders Pope's quote shown to the left says it perfectly.

Is that the reality of today? Should we not have expectations of doctors to perform their surgeries properly? Should we not have the expectations of lawyers to represent their clients properly? Should the real expectation be on myself to research, investigate and/or learn all *these professions myself... **Probably not.** And, when any of these professionals screw up, should they be held accountable? **Probably so.** Did everything that happened to me happen for a reason? **Perhaps...** Have I learned the lessons to eliminate my negative attitude and shift it to help others? Because of all that happened in my past, do I now have a better and shifted attitude? Definitely Yes! I believe I am now, according to Alexander Pope, "BLESSED!"*

The loss of my house, my money, my mental well-being has just better prepared me to deal better with life's challenges and accept this as part of my journey.

It is because I have lived life and managed to get through and experience each of those ups and downs that have brought me to where I am today. I have finally moved to my ultimate dream destination, and live with the waves crashing beside my window in Cabo San Lucas, Mexico. I surround myself with happy, positive people. I enjoy speaking to groups about the benefits of MER, and now that I'm a Master Practitioner, I guide others in discovering their own passion and purpose. I volunteer my free time to work with various charities, donate and attend fundraising events, and as a member of the American Legion Auxiliary, I paint children's faces when their parents are being deployed and when they come

I'm not short. I'm just more down to earth than other people. ~ Wallpago back from overseas.

I am no longer feeling 'STUCK" in any relationship. I choose who I want to spend my time with, go out with, and don't feel obligated or guilty about moving on. I'm friends with my old boyfriends and I am finally able to live a life of passion and purpose again. I can finally live an empowered life because I have gained the necessary tools to overcome those hiccups that are bound to keep popping up.

I am no longer stuck in my own sadness. I am able to share the tools I have learned along my journey and believe MY new purpose is to help others reclaim their own passion and purpose in life.

Purpose - as long as someone is doing something, they are either doing it with or without intention. I use quantum linguistics, a tool to uncover the deeper issues. Most people argue over their reality, if I loosen up the boundaries to the problem, they can then get ready to release it. In order for a person to take a problem and make it real, they need to be ignoring one of the Cartesian coordinates. Once they understand which quadrant is missing, they can admit that their problem isn't real.

As others have inspired me to write this book, I hope that it inspires others who are stuck in life, to take action. I truly want to become a beacon of light and help others empower their own lives and learn how to "let go"

There are two types of people who will tell you that you cannot make a difference in this world: Those who are afraid to try and those who are afraid you will succeed. ~ Ray Goforth of their past. So, they too, can also achieve their most magnificent dreams.

I'm so happy that you have gotten this far in the book.
Here is another gift for you!

This is a **$1500^ OFF** Coupon
for either a
Personal Breakthrough or MER Session.

Go to: http://bit.ly/LetitGo_Schedule
Sign up for an Initial Consultation today and
find out if YOU Qualify!

$1,500^ OFF

MER SESSION or
PERSONAL BREAKTHROUGH

^Some restrictions apply. See website for terms and details.

A big challenge in life —is to be YOURSELF in a world that is trying to make you like everyone else.

We all have an unsuspected reserve of strength inside that emerges when life puts us to the test.

~ Isabel Allende

"One can choose to go back toward safety
or forward toward growth.
Growth must be chosen again and again;
fear must be overcome again and again."

~ Abraham Maslow

Chapter 12

~What IS a Personal MER® Breakthrough?~

Y ou can also download both of these diagrams in color from our website in the book bonus section, or by typing in the following URLs:

http://bit.ly/16STEPS and http://bit.ly/MER_image

MER® Timeline Therapy

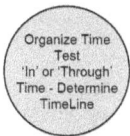

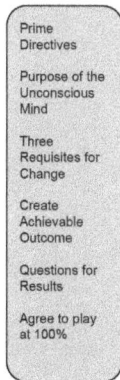

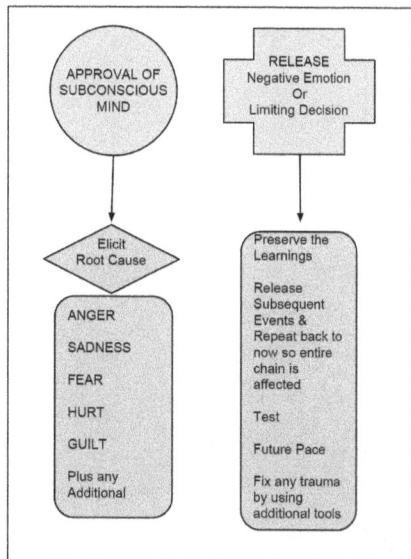

Organize Time
Test
'In' or 'Through'
Time - Determine
TimeLine

Discussion of
Necessities
&
Process
Overview

Prime
Directives

Purpose of the
Unconscious
Mind

Three
Requisites for
Change

Create
Achievable
Outcome

Questions for
Results

Agree to play
at 100%

APPROVAL OF
SUBCONSCIOUS
MIND

RELEASE
Negative Emotion
Or
Limiting Decision

Elicit
Root Cause

ANGER

SADNESS

FEAR

HURT

GUILT

Plus any
Additional

Preserve the
Learnings

Release
Subsequent
Events &
Repeat back to
now so entire
chain is
affected

Test

Future Pace

Fix any trauma
by using
additional tools

The full Personal Breakthrough is up to 16 steps, and usually takes between 8-12 hours. It can be done over one or two days. The MER® section of the therapy is detailed in the previous diagram.

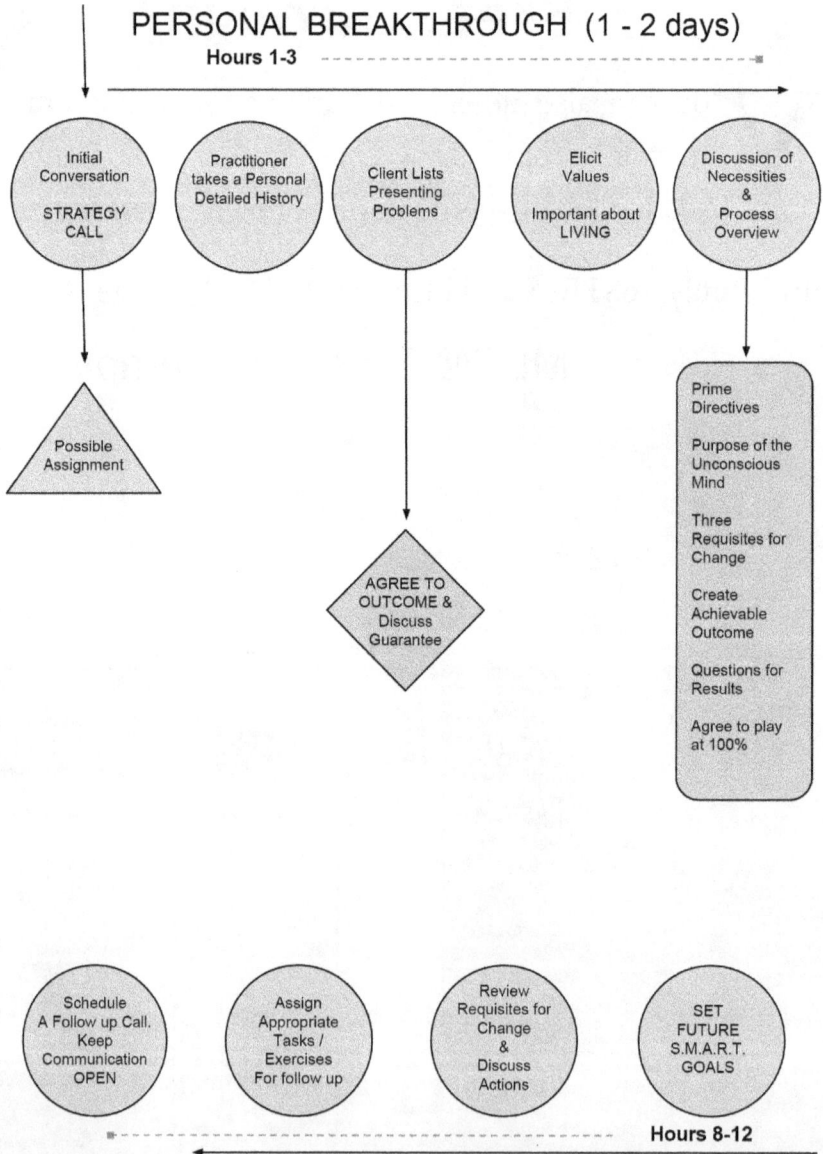

PERSONAL BREAKTHROUGH (1 - 2 days)

Hours 1-3

Initial Conversation

STRATEGY CALL

Practitioner takes a Personal Detailed History

Client Lists Presenting Problems

Elicit Values

Important about LIVING

Discussion of Necessities & Process Overview

Possible Assignment

AGREE TO OUTCOME & Discuss Guarantee

Prime Directives

Purpose of the Unconscious Mind

Three Requisites for Change

Create Achievable Outcome

Questions for Results

Agree to play at 100%

Schedule A Follow up Call. Keep Communication OPEN

Assign Appropriate Tasks / Exercises For follow up

Review Requisites for Change & Discuss Actions

SET FUTURE S.M.A.R.T. GOALS

Hours 8-12

Life is a challenge - Meet it! Life is a dream - Realize it! Life is a game- Play it! Life is love - Enjoy it!

PERSONAL BREAKTHROUGH (continued)

Hours 3-6

- Establish Patterns & Greater/Greatest Problem

- Organize Time Test 'In' or 'Through' Time - Determine TimeLine

- APPROVAL OF SUBCONSCIOUS MIND

- RELEASE Negative Emotion Or Limiting Decision

- Establish A Resource Anchor

- TEST & Find Safety

- Elicit Root Cause

ANGER

SADNESS

FEAR

HURT

GUILT

Plus any Additional

Preserve the Learnings

Release Subsequent Events & Repeat back to now so entire chain is affected

Test

Future Pace

Fix any trauma by using additional tools

Check if the Greater Problem is Gone?

Parts Integration
Chaining Anchors
Swish
Prime Concerns
Like to Dislike
Phobias
PTSD

Now, Is the Greater Problem Gone?

Hours 6-8

TEST & Future Pace

- Hypnosis & Pendulum if needed

- Complete The Change
Revisit Desired Outcomes

- RE-Elicit Values

Don't fear failure. Fear being in the exact same place next year as you are today.

If any of this book has resonated with you and you would like more information. Please visit my website at: www.LetitGo-MER.com.

Because my mission is to help as many people as possible to get UNSTUCK, For a limited time, Just because you purchased this book, I will be offering ALL my readers a Complimentary Strategy Call*

*With a $299 refundable deposit - See website for details.

Be stubborn about your goals, and flexible about your methods.

Chapter 13

~Exercises, Tools & Resources~

If any of this book has resonated with you, I advise you take one of the sessions or trainings that can be found on my website. Here are some key questions to ask yourself.

1. Is something from your past still bothering you and you can't seem to shake it off or "let it go"? How does it affect you in any of the following areas of your life?

Career

Relationship

Family

Health/Fitness

Spirituality

2. Are you interested in discovering the root cause or first event that initiated a negative emotion or limiting decision that has interfered with being successful in the law of attraction or positive affirmations?

3. Are you holding onto a Negative emotion including:

Anger

Sadness

Fear

Hurt

Guilt or

Frustration?

4. Is it time to remove a Limiting Decision that you believe in that has become a problem or self sabotaging behavior? Some beliefs include and aren't limited to: "I'm not good enough," "I can't make enough money," "I don't deserve a great relationship," "People are out to get me," "I'm not able to get ahead," etc.

5. Do you feel you are always chasing time, can't catch up, always late? This may require a simple tweak by switching the internal direction of your timeline from "IN" time to "THROUGH" time.

6. Do you have too much anxiety about the future causing you the inability to function normally?

(I suggest: A personal breakthrough to discover the direction and location of your timeline, remove all negative emotions and limiting beliefs/decisions, putting events into your future to release anxiety and create a positive outcome)

There is an abundance of NLP tools that can be used to reprogram your habits, thoughts, values and strategies once you take control and become the cause, not the

Life's challenges are not suppose to paralyze you, they're supposed to help you discover WHO YOU ARE.
~ Bernice Johnson Reagon

effect of any situation.

Through a very thorough background question and answer period, we can use linguistic presuppositions based on your current language patterns to determine and recognize what your unconscious mind assumes to be true. Once identified, we can help to create new, better internal representations of those beliefs, habits, patterns, thoughts, actions, and feelings.

SEVERAL OF THE NLP TOOLS WE USE INCLUDE:

Utilizing Sub-Modalities

Mapping Across - Like to Dislike

Swish Patterns - Dissociative Techniques

Parts Integration - Perceptual Positions

Anchoring - Simple, Stacked/Resource, Collapsing, Chaining

Strategies

Values

Hierarchy of Ideas and Several Language Patterns

Beauty begins the moment you decide to be yourself.

~ Coco Chanel

Can you remember a time when you felt completely positively motivated to sign up for a class, seminar or training event that would benefit YOU? A specific time? As you think back to that time, what was the very first thing that caused you to take action? Was it something you saw, heard, or felt? After you saw, heard or felt that first, what was the very next thing that happened to cause you to take action and sign up to move forward? Did you picture something, hear something in your mind, say something to yourself or have a certain feeling or emotion?

Think back about how you felt...

Feelings and emotions are the result of the images we put in our minds. We generally communicate and talk in a certain way based on our current emotion. Throughout most of our lives we have created a set of memories and beliefs based on specific past events. These memories and beliefs are what we call the "internal representation" of our reality, or our own "TRUTH". We hold it in our minds as "fact", although we just perceive it as a truth or fact. Our perceived reality of the world has a positive or negative effect on our current state of mind. Our state of mind affects our physiology (our actions and behaviors). Therefore, how we act, and what we say is in direct

Don't mistake silence for weakness. Smart people don't plan big moves out loud.

correlation to how we perceive reality as we believe it to be true.

Our reality is a mental construction of Space, Time, Matter, and Energy.

We construct our reality by what we observe. We observe with our minds. Observations are measurements. All the time in our lives can be visited and evaluated in our mind's eye through what we call a timeline. Measurements transform nothing into something. We also make measurements through our language. When our language does not generate the positive desired behavior, we may need to make a shift in the way we talk in order to gain the desired result. Everyone is entitled to their own reality, not everyone wants the shift. We are meant to go through certain realities and lessons. That is how we become the people we are today.

> EVERYONE IS ENTITLED TO THEIR OWN REALITY, NOT EVERYONE WANTS THE SHIFT.

Confidence is silent. Insecurities are loud.

~Language Patterns~

First, I'm going to tell you about language patterns, and how they affect what we attract into our lives. I'm going to share with you my favorite exercise, the one that initially made the most significant difference in the way I talk to others and talk to myself. Beliefs and the way we express them can limit our potential. I'm going to tell you this just because by changing a few key words, and asking ourself some key questions, we can train our unconscious minds to do and seek out what we really want instead of attracting what we are trying to avoid.

Modal Operators "set the frame" for modifying the verb that follows the Modal Operator:

1. "I must change." – A frame of necessity

2. "I have to change." – A frame of necessity

3. "I desire to change." – A frame of desire

4. "It is possible to change." – A frame of possibility

5. "I can change." – A frame of possibility

6. "I choose to change." – A frame of choice

In each of the above examples the Modal Operators affect or modulate the action of the verb, and hence perception. It does so because we have put the Modal Operator in a meta-position to our primary state of changing. This means the Modal Operator term

Peace is the result of retraining your mind to process life as it is, rather that as you think it should be.

~ Wayne Dyer

meta-states the verb and so determines the frame for the verb. In NLP we say that "all meaning is context dependent," and Modal Operators set the context, the frame, in determining the meaning of the verb.

In addition to limiting the options we have available, such beliefs can also make us feel negatively towards ourselves. Such beliefs can make us feel inadequate if we don't follow through on them. For example, if there is something we believe we "should" do (say, exercise regularly) and we don't do it then we can feel guilty or feel that we have somehow failed. Such beliefs create a gap between expectation and reality.

In order to help identify if the action governed by this belief is acceptable, ask the question: "what would happen if I did/did not do this?" By making the consequences of not following the rule explicit and examining the consequences you can determine how important the rule is, in what circumstances the rule does not need to be followed, and even if the rule needs to be followed at all.

This method of thinking is the basis of the scientific method. Many great discoveries and advancements in peoples thinking have come about by asking the question "What would happen if?"

We all have language patterns, the way we talk, the way we write. We have adapted these patterns from our interactions and experiences with others. It's how we

The secret to living well and longer is: eat half, walk double, laugh triple and love without measure.
~ Tibetan Proverb

perceive the world around us. Limiting beliefs can be identified with the words "cannot" or "impossible".

In order to see through a belief statement, replace "I can't" with "I won't". This shows that it is a choice and not an absolute fact. For example, changing "I can't give a speech in front of a thousand people" to "I won't give a speech in front of a thousand people" clarifies that you are making a choice. It may be a valid choice — giving a speech in front of a thousand people is a difficult task — but it isn't impossible.

Another approach to take is to ask yourself "what would happen if I did?" or "what stops me?" or "how do I stop myself?" These questions help further clarify what is preventing you from achieving something and can give insight into how to move forward.

For example, I could have started off writing this book with what may have sounded like a complaining, negative attitude that may not have been received in a welcoming fashion. I may have started out by saying

"I hate my life, I feel like it **WON'T** *get any better. I* **CAN'T** *do anything about it right now. I* **SHOULDN'T** *even be alive. People don't respect me. I* **AM NOT** *good enough. I am* **UNABLE TO** *do the things I want to do, and It's* **IMPOSSIBLE** *to get ahead."*

I have bolded to emphasize certain words so you can

recognize the patterns. Using words that limit our behaviors such as: **"WON'T," "CAN'T," "SHOULDN'T," "DON'T," "AM NOT, "UNABLE TO," AND "IMPOSSIBLE".** These **INACTION** words put a block in our unconscious minds that prevents us from consciously being able to do, get, or have what we really want. Read through the end of this section and then try the exercise yourself. Use as a reference the diagram on the following page. A color version can be downloaded at: http://bit.ly/ModalOperators

If you get tired, learn to rest not to quit.

Almost every successful person begins with two beliefs:
The future can be better than the present, and I have the power to make it so.

MODAL OPERATORS

INACTIVE
WORDS:

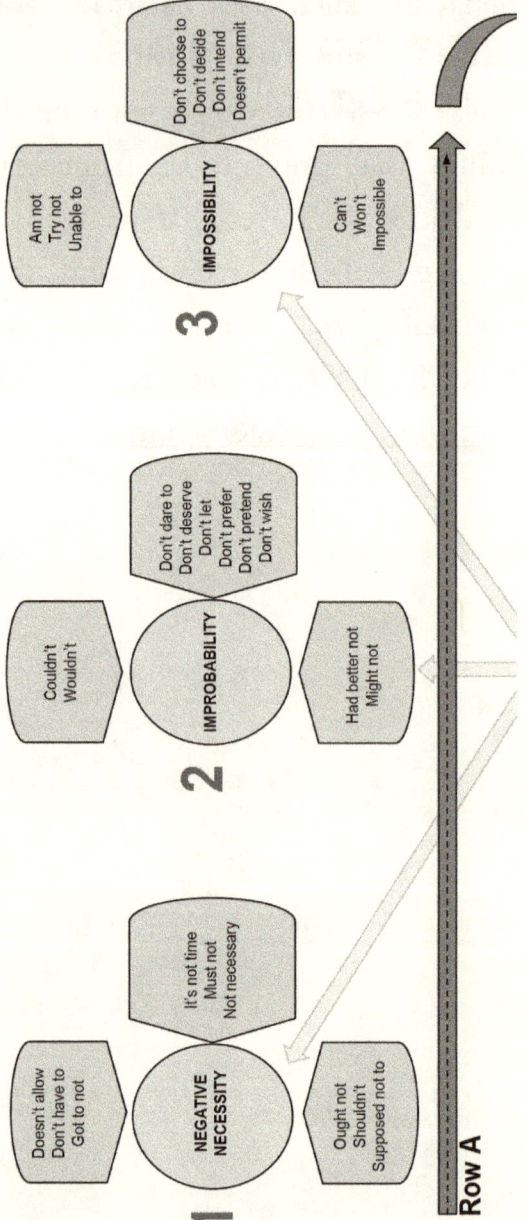

1 NEGATIVE NECESSITY

Doesn't allow
Don't have to
Got to not

It's not time
Must not
Not necessary

Ought not
Shouldn't
Supposed not to

2 IMPROBABILITY

Couldn't
Wouldn't

Don't dare to
Don't deserve
Don't let
Don't prefer
Don't pretend
Don't wish

Had better not
Might not

3 IMPOSSIBILITY

Am not
Try not
Unable to

Don't choose to
Don't decide
Don't intend
Doesn't permit

Can't
Won't
Impossible

Row A

ACTIVE WORDS:

Row B

4 NECESSITY

- Allow
- Have to
- Got to

- It's time
- Must
- Necessary

- Ought to
- Should
- Supposed to

5 PROBABILITY

- Could
- Would

- Dare to
- Deserve
- Let
- Prefer
- Pretend
- Wish

- Had better
- Might

6 POSSIBILITY

- Am
- Try
- Able to

- Choose to
- Decide
- Intend
- Permit

- Can
- Will
- It is possible

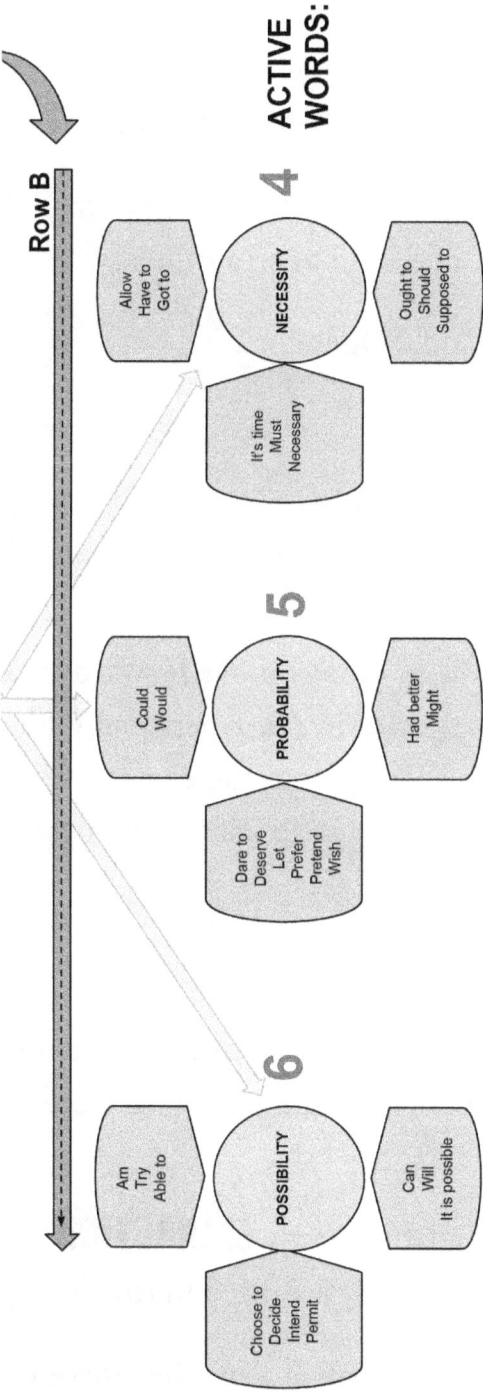

live with no excused and travel with no regrets.

{EXERCISE 1}

Model Operators - I'm going to show you how to switch your thinking to make the **IMPOSSIBLE... POSSIBLE!**

How to go from an <u>inactive</u> state of mind into a state of <u>action</u>. It's very powerful and used to create energy.

See the diagram called Modal Operators.

Notice the two rows: A & B

Row A has a list of **INACTION** words

Row B has a list of **ACTION** words

The key to this exercise is to always move forward in a clockwise way and always end on #6. I personally like to put in as many words as I can into the correct order and make a long flowing paragraph to encourage myself. (this is shown in example #3)

Here is <u>How</u> to do the exercise:

- Ask yourself, "What's the problem?" Take a few minutes to jot down your answers on a piece of paper...

- Find and circle all the words of **INACTION** on your piece of paper. (they are listed in row A)

- Find the corresponding word on the provided diagram and note in which of the 1-6 sections it is located.

- From the next chronological section, choose a word and create a new sentence and then do the same for each proceeding section until you have recreated your sentence with a word from #6 (Possibility)

Here are a few Examples of this exercise:

EXAMPLE 1

1) Determine the problem:

I **CAN'T** make enough money to make my wife happy.

2) Recognize the limitation or **INACTION** word(s)

CAN'T is in Row A - Section 3 "Impossibility"

3) Choose any word(s*) from sections 4, 5 & 6
section 4 (**IT'S TIME**),
section 5 (**WISH AND/OR COULD**),
& section 6 (**IT IS POSSIBLE**)

4) Shift the original sentence from **INACTION** words to words of **ACTION** to create Necessity:

Using Section 4 - **IT'S TIME** to start looking at more employment options

5) Shift the original sentence from **INACTION** words to words of **ACTION** from section 5 to create Probability:

I **WISH** my wife **COULD** have everything she always wanted.

6) Shift the original sentence from **INACTION** words to words of **ACTION** from section 6 to create <u>Possibility</u>:

IT IS POSSIBLE I can ask for a raise, or I will find a higher paying job

EXAMPLE 2

1) State the problem

My parents **DON'T ALLOW** me to go out with my friends

2) Recognize the limitation or **INACTION** word(s)

DON'T ALLOW is in Row A -
Section 1 "<u>Negative Necessity</u>"

3) Choose any word(s*) from Row 1 sections (2 or 3) + Row B sections 4, 5, and 6 –
section 2 (**WOULDN'T**), then,
section 4 (**OUGHT TO**),
section 5 (**MIGHT**), &
section 6 (**WILL**)

4) Shift the original sentence from section 2 to get out of "<u>Negative Necessity</u>"

My parents **WOULDN'T** intentionally do anything to upset me

5) Shift the original sentence from **INACTION** words to words of **ACTION** from sections 4 & 5 to create

'Necessity' & 'Probability'

I **OUGHT** to invite him to come along a few times so they **MIGHT** understand it's just a hang out and study group

6) Shift the original sentence from **INACTION** words to words of **ACTION** from section 6 to create <u>Possibility</u>: (it is not necessary to put in a word from section 5 again, and it can also be included)

By taking them along they **MAY** get bored and or feel over protective since no other parents are included...then they **WILL CHOOSE TO** allow me to attend on my own

Now, put it all together...

All words in order in a long sentence to create action: Instead of using negative language patterns as:

1) My parents **DON'T ALLOW** me to go out with my friends

One could choose to use the following instead:

I **DON'T** wish to upset and fight with my parent, so, I **WON'T** aggravate them unnecessarily. **IT'S TIME** that I **SHOULD** ask them if they **MIGHT PREFER** to join me. Then they can **CHOOSE TO** come with me or **CHOOSE TO PERMIT** me to go on my own.

* More than 1 word in a section is okay, keep writing or including them in your sentences. Just never go backwards into the previous section.

I figured that if I said it enough, I would convince the world that I really was the greatest.

~ Muhammad Ali

~What's Your Personality Type? ~

(The following is taken directly from one of Dr. Joe Dispenza's YouTube Videos and absolutely pertinent to what this book talk about)
You Tube Video can be found at http://bit.ly/DrJoe_negative_thoughts

Have you ever been told that the way you think has something to do with your life?

How about that feelings and emotions are the end result of past experiences? Did you know that you can remember certain events better because of the way they made you feel?

Do you know how to control your emotional responses or reactions to external experiences?

If you don't, someone at one point has probably asked, "What's wrong?"

And your response was, "I'm in a mood... Something happened to me FOUR HOURS AGO."

That means that you are living by the same emotional reaction.

If you keep that same refractory period going on for weeks or months, that's called a temperament.

Someone may have asked you, "Why are you SO angry?"

If your response was, "Well, this thing happened to me NINE MONTHS AGO..."

You are living by one very long refractory period.

And, if you keep that emotional response going on for years, it's called a personality trait. My mom said that I'm not as smart as my brother... 26 YEARS AGO. So now, I'm just shy, or insecure.

Most people wear their emotions layer by layer and they start to believe that is who they really are. If you continue to think in the past, what do you think are creating more of ?

Most people spend most of their time preparing themselves for the worst case scenario and protecting themselves from it. Basically, they are trying to predict the future from the past and if they are not correct they have anxiety, neurosis, and insomnia. Is your mind stuck and missing out on change and possibility?

Let me give you an example: As I mentioned earlier in this book, the man I've been dating throughout my entire transformational journey has mentioned to me a number of times that he is hurt by many of my actions. My response is that I am not doing anything TO him, and he is in charge of his own emotions. He insists that everything that I do in my own life affects him. Where I go and who I interact with.

His mind is spinning with all the worst case scenarios of what I could possibly be doing and what might happen. So, when we talk, even before we have a discussion about

Affirmation without discipline is the beginning of delusion.

~ Jim Rohn

what is going on in my life, he is already overwhelmed, irritated, and seems surprised with almost anything I bring up or mention.

I have learned to enjoy the moments I do spend with this man, no longer planning for the future, no longer bringing up the past. I now know and understand that our relationship has run its course, I have grown, transformed and changed my perception. I no longer look towards a future or the possibility of "US". And, I'm absolutely okay with that.

Some say, just break it off. I feel like we still have a bond and a connection. If either of us needed anything we would still be there for one another. I believe that I will and would make every effort to become available to any person, friend or family who reached out to me who is in need.

Although I very much enjoy his company and friendship, my emotions and desires of wanting to spend the rest of my life with this man have transformed into a pure love of gratitude and appreciation for being a huge part of my journey.

I understand more than ever that I cannot create a positive and fulfilling future by holding onto the emotions of the past. Humans can make thoughts more real than anything else. MER® works on the subconscious mind and asks open ended questions. Reminding ourselves of what we deeply want and who we want to be. These questions will cause our brains to find different and new patterns.

Through the process of MER®, your mind can move your body from a state of survival to a state of gratitude and creation. With these new thinking patterns your body can now live in the future and not in the past. This new state of being creates a new personality. And a new personality will help to create your new personal reality.

Several studies show different personalities are better for different jobs and tasks.

Take this quick 10 question quiz that will show you what type of person you are and which type of person is best for you to interact with in order to achieve your particular goals. Several studies show different personalities are better for different jobs and tasks. Go to: LetitGo-MER.com Book Bonuses, or download at: http://bit.ly/LGMER_personality, take the test, and get your immediate results.

Every action and feeling is preceded by a thought.

~ James Allen

~Are You Living a Life According to Your True Values?~

Did you know you can adjust the order of your personal values? If your number one value is FREEDOM, and are not happy in one of the areas of your life where you feel trapped, stuck in a cubicle all day, and FREEDOM is not one of the top 4 subconscious values, then you will need to adjust the submodalities of your values to get in alignment with your higher self.

Go to our website and watch the video on how to elicit Your Personal Values.

http://letitgo-mer.com/about/our-team/over-view-and-videos/

Or contact us for additional instructions.

~Affirmations and Positive Quotes~

I'm sure you noticed that throughout this book the sides are filled with positive affirmations and quotes. If you do nothing else, flip through and read them once a day. Allow them to inspire new thoughts and dreams, transfer your mood and give you hope. Write your own personal quotes and affirmations that are meaningful to you . Review, read and repeat them to yourself daily and before you know it, you will feel an internal change. Post your experiences on our FB Community page.

Affirmations are our mental vitamins, providing the supplementary positive thoughts we need to balance the barrage of negative events and thoughts we experience daily. ~ Tia Walker

~Final Thought~

I hope you have found value in what I have shared with you on my personal journey to empowerment.

Remember, we are like the artichoke and at the beginning of our journey, letting go of our core beliefs at the root cause of our negative emotions seems daunting. As we get closer to the heart of our problems, daily issues and challenges are continually brought to the surface, causing us to dive in deeper or further back to find the cause and learn the necessary lessons of life. While these challenges will continue to appear, because we have the tools, letting go and eliminating the triggers will gradually become easier.

Now that you have become aware of the tools, and if you learn how to use them, or find the support and guidance to walk you through each of the steps, your journey of transformation can begin. You will finally start to see and feel like you are able to thrive in all aspects of your life, empowered and confident to take new roads and grow in the direction of your true passion and purpose.

Then, you too, once you take the steps can live every day as if it's the best day of your life!

Join my FaceBook Group where you can post victories, ask questions, obtain additional guidance on how to

To give someone a blessing is the most significant affirmation we can offer.

~ Henri Nouwen

overcome challenges, inspire others, and share your own personal journey to empowerment!

May you feel the light shine upon you.

May you find comfort in knowing there is hope.

May you grasp the tools and support that is available to you, and

May you finally live a truly happy, passionate and purposeful life.

Congratulations on taking the first step to Empowerment!

~ Liana

~Reference Information~

1. *NLP* – *Neuro Linguistic Programming - how to use language to achieve a desired and specific result.*

Neuro: The Nervous system where we process everything to do with the 5 senses

Linguistic: Non verbal and verbal communication in which "things" are given labels and meanings. Pictures, Sounds, Feelings, Tastes, Smells, Names, Words.

Programming: The ability to use specific tools within our communication style to achieve a specific results.

2. *MER* – *Mental and Emotional Release Therapy - A fast and effective way of letting go of negative emotions (fear, anger, sadness, hurt, and guilt). It utilizes visualization, hypnotherapy, and NLP to treat depression, trauma, phobias, or other major or minor "stuff".*

3. *Trigger WARNING!!* *This chapter may be a trigger warning for victims of sexual assault. If you find yourself reacting negatively to this chapter, please pause and utilize the tools found on the LetitGo-MER. com website (book bonuses & video samples) where I show you how to overcome feelings of anxiety and how to find your safe place. Search for 'floating higher up and further back'.*

4. *timeline - A timeline is a display of a list of events in chronological order. Most timelines use a linear scale, in which a unit of distance is equal to a set amount of time. To elicit your personal timeline, go to http://bit.ly/overview_videos*

5. *S.M.A.R.T. Goals - (Specific, Measurable, Attainable, Realistic, Timely)*

6. *Secondary Gain - The advantage that occurs secondary to a stated or real illness. An example may be someone who does not want to get better because they will lose their financial medical disability benefits.*

7. *PTSD - Post Traumatic Stress Disorder: is a mental disorder that can develop after a person is exposed to a traumatic event, such as sexual assault, warfare, traffic collisions, or other threats on a person's life*

8. *Emotional Intelligence - The capacity to be aware of, control, and express one's emotions, and to handle interpersonal relationships judiciously and empathetically.*

9. *Ho'oponopono - A Hawaiian practice of reconciliation and forgiveness. To make it right with the ancestors, or to make right with the people with whom you have relationships.*

Every success story is a tale of constant adaption, revision and change.
~ *Richard Branson*